The 38 Letters from J.D. Rockefeller to his son

The letters written by Rockefeller to his son imparting his perspectives, ideology, and wisdom to his son.

Compiled and Translated by

G. Ng

Edited by M. Tan

2nd Edition

Foreword

There were times of the very low, there were times of the very high. But what goes up, must come down.

In compiling this book, a lot of the stories and letter written greatly resonated with me. As you read through the letters, empty your cup and read them with a set of clear perspective.

For it allows me to be guided, I hope it is for you as well.

To all my failures and rejections, you may have thrown me down, but you will never strip me off the passion I have for entrepreneurship.

For it is with my loved one that stands by me, I ought to bring about what I truly seek.

LETTER

1

Starting points do not determine your end point
Our destiny is determined by our actions, not by our origins.

People who are privileged but have no power are a waste, while those who are educated but uninfluenced are a pile of worthless rubbish.
(Men of privilege without power are waste-material. Men of enlightenment without influence are the poorest kind of rubbish.)

July 20, 1897

Dear John:

You hope that I can sail with you forever, this sounds great, but I am not your eternal captain. God created feet for us to let us walk on our own.

Maybe you are not ready to go alone, but you need to know that the challenging and magical business world that I am in is the starting point of your new life. You will start from there in order to participate in the feast of life that you have never enjoyed before and that relates to your future. As for how you use the knives and forks that are placed in front of you, and how you taste every dish served by the angel of destiny is entirely up to you.

Of course, I expect you to stand out from the crowd in future and outdo me. However, I have decided to keep you by my side, because

I want to bring you to a higher starting point in life, so that you can indulge in the rapid opportunities without having to face obstacles.

Of course, there is nothing worth showing off or for you to feel gratified about, and you do not need to be grateful. The founding belief of the United States of America is that all human beings are created equal, but this equality is only present in the context of rights and laws. It has nothing to do with economic and cultural advantages. Think of our world as a high mountain. When your parents live on the peak of the mountain, you are destined to not live at the foot of the mountain; likewise when your parents live at the foot of the mountain, you are destined to not live on the peak of the mountain. In most cases, the status of parents will determine the starting point of their child's life.

But this does not mean that everyone has a different starting point and life outcomes. In this world, there is never a saying of inheriting wealth or poverty, same goes to inheriting success or failure. The only truth is that as long as you work hard enough, you will succeed. I firmly believe that our destiny is determined by our actions, not by our origins.

As you know, when I was young, my family was very poor. I remember that the books I read when I was in high school were bought by my kind neighbours. In the beginning of my career as a bookkeeper, I was only earning a weekly salary of 5 dollars. But it was only through unremitting efforts that have enabled me to establish an enviable oil kingdom. In the eyes of others, this may seem to be a legend, but I think it is the reward for my perseverance and hard work from the god of destiny.

John, opportunities will always be unequal, but the results prove otherwise. In history, whether in politics or businesses, (especially in businesses), there has been many examples of successful people who started from scratch. They have had only a few opportunities because of poverty, but they eventually achieved fame because of their past struggles. However, history has also been filled with examples of rich children who were privileged but have failed in life. According to a study that was conducted in Massachusetts on 17 wealthy people, it was revealed that none of their children left the world wealthy.

A long time ago, there was a story in society that satirized the incompetence of rich children. It mentioned that in a small bar in Philadelphia, a guest was talking about a millionaire when he said, "He is a self-made millionaire." "Yeah," a smarter man next to him replied, "He inherited 20 million dollars, but now he is only left with a million."

This is a distressing story but in our society today, the rich children are caught between advancing and retreating. Many of them are destined to be sympathetic and pitiful, and even, go to hell.

The glory and success of the family cannot guarantee the future of its children and grandchildren. I admit that the early advantage is really helpful, but it does not guarantee them a victory in the end. I have thought about this distressing problem for rich children more than once. I feel that once rich children begin taking advantage of their family success, they will have little opportunity to learn and develop the skills needed for survival. People of poorer backgrounds will actively develop their creativity, abilities, while also cherishing and seizing various opportunities because they urgently need to rescue themselves. I have also observed that the kind of ambition of the rich children have, often lacks the motivation and attributes the poor, hence they resort to praying for their own success.

Therefore, when you and your sisters were very young, I deliberately concealed the fact that I was well off. I instilled many values such as frugality and personal struggle in you because I know that the quickest way to harm someone is to give them money. It can make people corrupt, depraved, arrogant, and cause them to lose their source of happiness. I cannot bury my beloved children with wealth, and foolishly make you all into one that is incompetent and only depends on the success of their parents.

A truly happy person is one who is able to enjoy his creation. Those of whom that are like sponges that only takes without giving will only lose happiness.

I believe that there is not one person in the world that does not long for a happy and luxurious life, yet not many people truly understand where it comes from. In my opinion, it does not come from wealthy blood, nor from a luxurious lifestyle, but from a luxurious character – the spirit of self-reliance. Only by looking at noble people who have won the respect of the world and exhibit charisma wherever they go, will we then know the worth of independence.

John, every move of yours will be of concern to me. However, as compared to being concerned, I am more confident in you, and I believe in your excellent character – a character that is more valuable than any wealth in the world, that will help you pave a good future, and lead a successful and fulfilling life

But you need to strengthen the belief that even though the starting point will affect the outcome, it does not determine it. Factors such as ability, attitude, character, ambition, method, experience, and luck play an extremely important role in life and the business world. Your life has just begun, but a battle of life is in front of you. I can deeply feel that you want to be the winner of this war, but you must know that everyone has the will to pursue victory, and only those who are determined and ready will win.

My son, the privileged but powerless people are a waste, while the educated but unaffected people are a pile of worthless garbage. Find your own way and God will help you!

Love,
Your Father

LETTER

2

Luck depends on planning

Everyone is a designer and architect of his own destiny.

I do not live by God-given luck, but I do-so by planning luck.

When waiting for luck, you must know how to guide luck; to design luck is to design life.

(He who marches in rank and file has already earned my contempt. He has been given a large brain by mistake, since for him the spinal cord would suffice.)

January 20, 1900

Dear John:

Some people are destined to be dazzling Kings or great men, because of their extraordinary talents, for example, Mr. McCormick, who has a head of luck and knows how to turn a harvester into a sickle for harvesting banknotes.

In my eyes, Old McCormick has always been an ambitious and commercially capable industrial giant. He used harvesting machines to liberate American farmers, and he also rose to the ranks to become one of the richest person in the United States. The French seem to like him more and praised him to be "the world's greatest contributor". Oh, this really is an unexpected reward.

This business genius who was once just an ordinary farm tool merchant once had an esoteric saying which went: "Luck is the remnant of design."

This phrase does sound quite brainy. Does it mean that luck is the result of planning and strategy? Or does it mean that luck is what remains after planning? My experience tells me that these two meanings exist. In other words, we create our own luck, and no action can eliminate it. Luck is the gospel that is difficult to get rid of in the planning process.

McCormick saw the true meaning of luck and opened his door to it. So, I am not surprised that McCormick harvesters' product can be sold all over the world.

However, in this world of ours, it is difficult to find people who are good at planning luck like Mr. McCormick, and it is difficult to find people who do not believe in yet understands luck.

In the eyes of ordinary people, luck is always innate. As long as they find out someone has attained success or have been promoted, they will say casually, with contempt: "This man's luck is so good, it is luck that helped him!" Such a person can never have a peek into the truth that makes one successful: everyone is a designer and architect of his own destiny.

I admit, just like a person cannot have no money, a person cannot have no luck. However, if you want to make a difference, you cannot wait for luck to patronize. My credo is: I do not live by God-given luck, but I do-so by planning luck. I believe that a good plan will affect luck, and in any case, it can successfully affect luck. My plan to turn competition into cooperation in the oil industry justified this.

Before the plan began, the oil refiners fought for their own interests, which led to a devastating competition between them. This kind of competition is certainly a boon for consumers, but falling oil prices are a disaster for oil refiners. At that time, the vast majority of refiners were a loss, and were successively sliding into bankruptcy.

I am well aware that if we were to be profitable again and make money forever, we must tame this industry and have everyone act rationally. I regard it as a responsibility, but it is very difficult to do, it requires a plan – a plan that places all the oil refining businesses under my control.

John, to be a good hunter in a profitable hunting ground, you need to think hard, be careful, be able to see all possible dangers and opportunities in things, as well as study all kinds of strategies that could endanger your dominance like a chess player. I thoroughly researched the situation and evaluated my strength. I decided to use the base camp of Cleveland as my first battlefield to launch a war in order to rule the oil industry. After conquering more than 20 competitors there, I moved quickly to open up a second battlefield until I conquered all of their opponents and established an oil industry and a new order.

Just like a commander on the battlefield, you must first know what kind of firearm to choose in order to be the most effective, before choosing your target. in order for me to successfully realize my plan to place the oil industry under my command, a thorough solution is needed. That's money. I needed a lot of money to buy those refineries that overproduce. But the amount of money on my hands was not enough to realize my plan, so I decided to form a joint stock company to attract investors from outside the industry. Soon we registered a standard oil company in Ohio with millions of assets, and the capital expanded significantly within three and a half years but deciding when to do it is a matter of knowledge.

Visionary businessmen are always good at finding opportunities in every disaster, and that's how I did it. Before we started our journey of conquest, the oil industry was in chaos and there was no hope at all. Ninety percent of the refiners in Cleveland had been crushed by the increasingly fierce competition. If they did not sell the factory, they can only watch themselves go extinct. This was the best time to acquire an opponent.

It seems unethical to take an acquisition at times like these, but it really has nothing to do with conscience. An enterprise is like a battlefield, and the purpose of strategic goals is to create the most beneficial state for oneself. For strategic considerations, the first target I chose to conquer was not a small company that was vulnerable, but the strongest opponent, Clark Payne. This company was well-known in Cleveland and were ambitious, as they wanted to acquire my star oil refinery.

But before the opponent decides, I will have to strike first to gain the upper hand. I took the initiative to meet the largest shareholder of Clark Payne, my old friend in middle school, Mr. Oliver Payne, and I told him that the chaotic and sluggish era of the oil industry should end in order to protect the industry that countless families depend on for survival. I wanted to build a huge, high-performance oil company, and welcomed him to join. My plan impressed Payne, and finally they agreed to sell the company for 400,000 dollars.

I know that Clark Payne is not worth that amount at all, but I did not reject them. Acquiring Clark Payne meant that I would gain the title of the world's largest oil refinery and will also serve as a strong pioneer in the industry to efficiently bring together the refiners in Cleveland.

This trick really worked. In less than two months, there were 22 competitors under the leadership of Standard Oil, which eventually made me the big winner of that acquisition battle. This gave me unstoppable momentum. In the following three years, I conquered oil refiners in Philadelphia, Pittsburgh, and Baltimore successively, and became the only master of the oil refining industry in the United States.

Come to think about it, am lucky if I were to only lament-on-my bad luck at that time and follow the crowd, I might have been conquered. But I planned my luck.

Anything can happen in this world, but nothing can happen without doing anything (reap without sowing). Those who blindly follow the crowd and rules, I view them with disdain. Their brains are entangled with wrong thoughts, as they think that it is worth being complacent just by being able to withdraw themselves.

John, for our good luck to continue, we must carefully plan our luck, and planning luck requires a good plan. A good plan must be a good design, and a good design must be able to play a role. You need to know that when designing a good design, you must first consider two basic prerequisites. The first condition is to know your goals, such as what you want to do, or even what kind of person you want to become; the second condition is knowing what resources you have, such as status, money, interpersonal relationships, and even abilities.

The order of these two basic prerequisites is interchangeable. You may have an idea and/or a goal before you start looking for goals that can be achieved from these resources, or you can also mix them together to form the third and fourth methods, such as having a certain goal and a certain resource. To achieve your goal, you need to selectively choose and create some resources, and also own some resources and a goal, to which afterwards you can adjust your goals accordingly

After adjusting the goal according to the resource or the goal, you have a foundation – you can conceive the design structure, and the rest is up to you to fill it with your means and time, while waiting for luck to come.

You need to remember that my son, designing luck is designing life. So, while you wait for luck, you need to know how to guide your luck. Give it a try.

Love,
Your Father

LETTER

3

Comparing Heaven and Hell

The greatest reward for our hard work is not what we get, but what we will become.

If you view work as a pleasure, life is heaven; if you view work as a duty, life is hell.

(With this faith we will be able to hew out of the mountain of despair a stone of hope.)

November 9, 1897

Dear John:

There is an allegory that is very meaningful and provided me with a lot of insights.

The fable said:

In ancient Europe, a man found himself in a wonderful place where he could enjoy everything in his afterlife. As soon as he stepped into the piece of music, someone who looked like a waiter came over and asked him: "Sir, do you have any needs? Here you can have everything you want: delicious food, all possible forms of entertainment and all kinds of pastimes, amongst them are many beautiful young women where you can enjoy as you please."

After listening to the waiter, the man was a little surprised, but very happy, as he happily thought to himself: "this is not my dream in the world!" Throughout the day he had been tasting all of the delicious food while enjoying the taste of beauty. However, one day, he was bored, so he said to the waiter: "I am bored from all of this and I need to do something. Can you find me a job to do?"

He did not expect that the answer he received was the waiter shaking his head: "Sorry, my sir, this is the only thing we can't do for you here. There is no work here for you."

The man was very frustrated and waved his hand angrily as he said, "This is really bad! Then I will just stay in hell!"

"Where do you think you're at", said the waiter gently.

John, this very humorous fable tells me that: Losing work means losing happiness. It is regrettable that some people only realize this after being unemployed, which is very unfortunate!

I am proud to say that I have never tasted unemployment. This is not my luck, because I never treat work as hard labour without fun, instead I found infinite happiness from work.

I think that work is a privilege, as it brings more than just sustaining life. Work is the foundation of all businesses, the source of prosperity, and the shaper of genius. Work makes young people work harder and do more than their parents no matter how rich they are. Work is expressed in the humblest forms and lays the foundation for happiness. A job helps to add flavours to life. But people must love work before it can return the biggest favours and achieve the greatest results.

When I first entered the business world, I often heard that a person who wants to climb to the peak needs to make a lot of sacrifices. However, as the years passed, I began to understand that many people who were climbing to the peak were not "paying the price." They work hard because they really like work. People who climb up in any industry are fully committed to what they are doing and are dedicated. Sincerely love the work you do; you will naturally succeed.

Loving work is a belief. With this faith, we can heave the desperate mountain into a rock of hope. A great painter said it well, "Pain will eventually pass, but beauty will last forever."

But some people are obviously not smart enough. They have ambitions but are too picky about their work. They are always looking for a "perfect" employer or job. The fact is that employers need punctual, honest, and hard-working employees. They only leaves the salary increase and promotion opportunities to those employees who work hard, are very loyal, extra zealous, and spend more time doing things, because they are running a business, not a charity; they need those who are more valuable.

No matter how great a person's ambitions are, he must at least begin before he can reach the peak. Once started, it is not difficult to progress. The more difficult or unpleasant the work is, the more urgent it is to accomplish it. The longer he waits, the more difficult and scarier it becomes. This is a bit like shooting a gun. The longer you aim, the lower the chance of you pulling the trigger.

I will never forget my first job – the experience of being a bookkeeper. At that time, although I had to go to work every day when the morning just begun, but that never let me lose interest in the job. Instead, it fascinated and delighted me. Even all the red tape in the office did not make me lose my passion for the job. As a result, the employer kept raising my salary.

Income is just a by-product of your work. Doing what you should do, accomplishing what you should do well, the ideal salary will come. And more importantly, the highest reward for our hard work is not what we get, but what we will become. Those who are mentally active do not just work hard to earn money; the real reason behind the passion for their work is far more noble– they are engaged in a fascinating career.

Honestly, I am an ambitionist. Since I was a child, I have wanted to be a wealthy man. For me, the Hewitt Tuttle company I worked at is was a good place to exercise my ability and give myself a try in the business. It is a provider of a variety of commodities, owns an iron ore, and operates two technologies which the company heavily relies on to generate profits, namely, railways and telegraphs that revolutionized the American economy. It has brought me into a fun, vast and splendid business world, and taught me to respect numbers and facts. It has also allowed me to see the power of the transportation industry and has cultivated the abilities and qualities that I should have as a businessman. All of these have played a great role in my future business. I can say that without the experience at Hewitt Tuttle, I may have taken many detours in my career.

Now, whenever I think of Mr. Hewitt & Tuttle, I cannot help but feel grateful in my heart. That period of time marked the beginning of my career and laid the foundation for my struggles. I am forever grateful for that three and a half years of experience.

So, I have never complained about my employer unlike some who might say, "We are nothing but just slaves, we are being suppressed by our employers, but they are standing tall while enjoying themselves in their beautiful villas; their safes are full with gold, and every dollar they have is obtained by exploiting honest workers like us." I don't know if these complainers want to be irregular (minority), but: Who gave you the opportunity to work? Who gave you the chance to build a family? Who gave you the possibility to develop yourself? If you realized they are exploiting you, why don't you end it by leaving for good?

The work bench is a type of attitude; it determines whether we are happy or not. In a group of stone masons who are doing the same job sculpting stone statues, if you were to ask them, "what are you doing here?" One of them might say, "You see, I am chiselling stone, and I can go home after chiselling this piece." This kind of person always treats work as a punishment, and the word he often spits out from his mouth is "tired".

Another person might say: "You see, I am making a statue. This is a very hard job, but the compensation is very high. After all, I have a wife and four children, and they need food and clothing." Regarding work as a burden, a sentence he often spits out from his mouth is "feeding his family".

The third person may put down the hammer and proudly point to the stone carving and say, "You see, I am making a work of art." This kind of person always takes pride in and enjoys his work and often cites: "this job is very meaningful."

Heaven and hell are created by ourselves. If you give meaning to your work, you will feel happy regardless of its size and you will feel fulfilled no matter what self-set results you have attained. If you don't like to do anything, even the simplest things will become difficult and boring. When you lament that this work is very tiring, despite not working hard, you will feel exhausted, in other words there is a huge difference. This is how things are.

John, if you view work as a pleasure, life is heaven; if you view work as a duty, life is hell. Reflect on your work attitude, it will make everyone happy.

Love,
Your Father

LETTER

4

Do it now
Opportunity comes from opportunity.

Bad habits can dictate us and determine success or failure. It is easy to develop, but it is difficult to serve.

Successfully putting a good idea into practice is more valuable than thinking about a thousand good ideas at home.

(To conquer you have need to do, to do again, ever to do! And your safety is insured.)

December 24, 1897

Dear John:

I always clearly remember the words of intelligent people. A wise man said it well, "Education covers many aspects, but it does not teach you anything." This wise man showed us a truth: if you do not take action, even the world most practical, beautiful, and viable philosophy will not work.

I have always believed that an opportunity comes from another opportunity as even the best ideas have flaws. Even if it is a very ordinary plan, if it is actually implemented and developed, it will be much better than a good plan that is abandoned halfway, because the former will be carried out consistently, but the latter has already been given up. So, I said that there is no secret to success. To achieve positive results in life, it is of course good to have extraordinary wisdom and special talents. There is nothing wrong with it. As long as you are willing to take active actions, you will be closer to success.

Unfortunately, many people have not remembered this biggest lesson, and as a result they have resulted to mediocrity. If you look at the ordinary people, you will find that they are all living passively, they always say much more than they do, or even do nothing. But almost all of them are good at finding excuses, they will find various excuse to procrastinate until they finally prove that this matter should not be, unable to or it is too late to be done.

Compared to this kind of person, I seem to be much smarter and cunning. Mr. Gates touted me as an active and spontaneous individual. I am happy to hear this because I have lived up to it. Positive action is another positive attribute of mine. I never like to talk in vain. Because I know that there is no result without action, and there is nothing in the world that is obtained just from thinking. As long as people are alive, they must consider taking action.

Many people admit that knowledge without experience is useless, but what is even more frustrating is that even if there is knowledge and wisdom but no action, everything is still empty talk. Action and adequate preparation can actually be seen as two sides of an object. We need to live modestly. Too much preparation but no action at all will only waste time eventually. In other words, everything must be done with limits. We cannot fall into the trap of continuous deliberation and planning but we must recognize the reality: no matter how detailed the plan is, we still cannot accurately predict the final outcome.

Of course, I do not deny that planning is very important. It is the first step to achieving favourable results, but planning is not, and cannot replace action. Just like playing golf, if you have not completed the first hole, you cannot progress to the second hole. Action solves everything. Without action, nothing will happen. We cannot buy fool proof insurance, but what we can do is make up our minds to fulfil our plan.

People who lack action have a bad habit: they like to maintain the status quo and refuse to change. I think this is a bad habit that is deceptive and self-destructive because everything is changing, just as people will live and die, there is nothing constant. But because of one's inner fear – the fear of the unknown, many people resist change. Even if the status quo does not satisfy him, he dares not take a step forward. If you look at the people who should have succeeded in their careers but did not, you know that it's not hard to sympathize with them.

Yes, everyone will be worried and scared when deciding on a huge event and will be faced with a dilemma. But the "action group" will use the determination to ignite the sparks in their soul, come up with various ways to fulfil their wishes, and gain the courage to overcome all kinds of difficulties.

Many people who lack action are naive and like to sit and wait for things to happen naturally. They naively think that others will care about their affairs. In actual fact, other than yourself, others will not be very interested in them. People are only interested in their own things. For example, in a business, the higher our profits, the more we must take the initiative to act, because the success or failure has little to do with others; they will not care. At this time, we'd better push it. If we are lazy, retreating, and waiting for others to take the initiative to kickstart things, the result will be disappointing.

Only by relying on oneself can a person then not let himself down and increase his chance to control his destiny. Smart people will only make things happen.

The most frustrating thing in life is that there are too many things to do, but there is not enough time. As a result, just by thinking about the plans that are unable to be carried out will only intimidate ourselves, and we end up not accomplishing anything. We must admit that with limited time, no one can complete everything. Smart people know that not all actions will produce good results, and only wise actions can bring meaningful results, so smart people will only learn from the work that has a positive effect in the future, and only concentrate on the work related that gives the greatest results. Hence, smart people always make the most valuable contribution and reap a lot of benefits.

To eat an elephant, you need to eat one bite at a time. Same goes to when you are doing something. If you want to accomplish everything at one go, you will only let the opportunity slip away. My motto is: *only takes unfair treatment for emergencies.*

Many people make themselves into a passive person. They want to wait until all conditions are perfect, that is, when the time is right, before taking action. Life is an opportunity at any time, but there is almost nothing perfect. Those passive people have a mediocre life, precisely because they must wait for everything to be 100% profitable and perfectly safe before doing something. This is a fool's approach. We must compromise in life and believe that what is in hand is the opportunity we need now, so that we can keep ourselves out of the quagmire of waiting forever before falling into action.

We pursue perfection, but there is no absolute perfection in life, only near perfection. If you wait until all conditions are perfect, you can only wait forever, and the opportunity will be given to others. Those who must wait until everything has been prepared will never leave home. To become the kind of person who "will do it now", you must stop daydreaming, and to always think of the present and start doing it now. Sentences such as "tomorrow", "next week", and "future" have the same meaning as "can never be done".

Everyone has a time when they lose confidence and doubts their abilities, especially in adversity. But people who really understand the art of action can overcome it with strong perseverance. They will tell themselves that everyone has failures, and when they fail miserably, they will tell themselves no matter how much preparation they have made and how long they think before they do it, will inevitably make mistakes. However, passive people do not regard failure as an opportunity for learning and growth, as they are always admonishing themselves: perhaps I really can't do it, so that is why I have lost my eagerness to participate in future activities.

Many people want their wishes to come true, but I regard it as a lie. It's a good idea to buy a dozen for a dime. The initial idea is just the beginning of a series of moves, and then comes the second stage of preparation, planning and the third stage of action. There is never a shortage of people with ideas in our world, but there are very few people who know how to successfully implement a good idea, which is more valuable than thinking about a thousand of good ideas at home.

The real basis people use to judge your ability is not how much you have in your head, but your actions. People trust down-to-earth people, and they will think: This person dares to say and do, he must know what the best course of action is. I haven't heard anyone being praised for not disturbing others, not acting, or having to wait for someone else to order things. Those leaders in the business sector, government, and military are very capable and willing people, who are 100% active. Those who stand on the side-lines and do nothing will never be leaders.

Whether it is an automatic spontaneous or a passive person, it is a habit. Habits are like ropes. We spin a rope every day, and finally it is too thick to break. The ropes of habit either lead us to the peak or lead us to the trough, which depends on whether our habits are good or bad. Bad habits can dictate us and determine success or failure. It is easy to develop, but it is difficult to serve. Good habits are difficult to develop, but they are easy to maintain.

To have the habit of doing now, the most important thing is to have a proactive spirit, get rid of the habit of being distracted, be determined to be a person of initiatives, be courageous in doing things, don't wait until everything is ready, there will never be absolute perfection. Cultivating the habit of action does not require special wisdom or special skills. You only need to work hard to let good habits bloom in life.

Son, life is a great battle. To win, you need to act, act again, and act forever! In this way, your safety can be guaranteed.

Merry Christmas! I think there is no better Christmas present than this letter to you at this time.

Love,
Your Father

LETTER

5

Be determined to compete

I do not go into war, but I destroy competitors.

Even if we lose, the only thing we should do is to lose gloriously

Crutches cannot replace strong and powerful feet; we have to stand on our own feet.

(These is no retreat but in submission and savvy! Our chains are forged! The war is inevitable, and let it come)

February 19, 1901

Dear John:

I have bad news to tell you that Mr. Benson passed away last night. I am very sad. Mr. Benson is an old rival and one of my few admired opponents. I am deeply impressed by his outstanding talent, tenacious will and grace.

To this day, I still remember the joke he made with me after our alliance, he said: "Mr. Rockefeller, you are a brilliant predator who is not soft-hearted. Losing to those bad guys would have made me very sad, because it was like a robbery, but playing with people like you, whether I win or lose, will make me happy."

At that time, I could not tell whether Mr. Benson was complimenting me or praising me. I told him: "Mr. Benson, if you can replace the predator with the conqueror, I think I will gladly accept it."

He smiled.

I admire the warriors who are still fighting bravely against their enemy, Mr. Benson is such a person. Before Benson became my enemy, I had just defeated the nation's largest railroad company, the Pennsylvania Railroad Company, and successfully subdued the nation's fourth and last large railroad company, Baltimore and Ohio Railroad Company. Just like that, together with my most loyal allies, the Erie Railroad Company and the New York Central Railroad Company, the four major railway companies in the United States have all become tools for me to tame.

At the same time, Standard Petroleum's oil pipelines extended bit by bit into the oil field, giving me absolute control over all major oil pipelines connecting oil wells and railroad trunk lines. Frankly speaking, at that time my influence had been extended to all corners of the oil industry such as oil extraction, refining, transportation, and markets. If I say that I have the power of life and death of oil producers and refiners, it is not a lie. I can make them wealthy or even make them worthless. But some people did ignore my authority, such as Mr. Benson.

Mr. Benson was an ambitious businessman who wanted to lay an oil pipeline from Bradford to Williamsport to save the independent oil producers who were afraid of being crushed by me and was also eager to get rid of me. Of course, the idea of making a fortune dominated him to bravely break into my territory.

This oil pipeline connecting north-eastern Pennsylvania to the west was laid forward at an alarming rate from the beginning. This brought me to attention. John, any competition is not an easy game, but a game full of vitality, requires close attention and constant decision-making, otherwise, you will lose if you are not careful.

Mr. Benson is creating trouble; I have to stop him. At first I used a set of unskilful methods to start a contest with Benson: I bought a long and narrow land along the Pennsylvania State border from north to south at a high price in an attempt to prevent Benson from moving forward, but Benson took a detour approach and avoided my heavy punches. As a result, I became an inactive landlord, and instead helped the farmers there become rich overnight. Then I used the power of my allies and asked the railway company to never let any oil pipelines cross their railways. Benson did the same and successfully broke through again. Finally, I wanted to use the power of the government to stop Benson, but without success, as I watched Benson become a hero.

I know that I have encountered a tough enemy to conquer, but he cannot shake my determination to compete, because the 110-mile pipeline is my biggest threat. If I let the crude oil flow there unimpeded, they will also acquire the supply line to New York. Then, Benson will replace me as the new owner of the New York oil refining industry, concurrently I will also lose ownership over the Bradford oil field. This is something I cannot allow.

Of course, I do not want to push them to the brink of desperation and trap them. My real goal is to get what I want without paying too high of a price – I can't let Benson come here and destroy the market that I built with all my efforts. This is my life's effort. So, when the Benson's company was about to start surging, I proposed to buy their stock. Unfortunately, they refused.

This angered many people. Mr. Oday, who was overseeing the company's pipeline transportation business, wanted to destroy it to punish those who did not know better. I despised such an evil idea, as only incompetent people will use such undesirable methods. I told Oday: "Kill your stupid idea! I never thought I would lose, but even if I lose, the only thing I should do is to lose gloriously."

If anyone can play tricks behind his back without being caught, he will almost certainly gain a competitive advantage. However, evil and unethical behavior is very dangerous, it will make him lose his dignity, and he may even go to jail. Any deceptive and unethical behavior cannot be sustained and cannot be a reliable corporate strategy. This only destroys the present situation, which will make the future increasingly difficult, and even impossible to gain another opportunity. We must pay attention to rules, because rules can create relationships, relationships will bring long-term businesses, good transactions will create more transactions, otherwise, we will end our good luck in advance.

As far as my nature is concerned, I do not meet competition, I destroy competitors. But I do not need a bright victory, I want to win it good, thorough, and decent. Just as Benson was proud and enjoying his success, I launched a series of offensives that made him difficult to parry. I sent someone to place a large amount of orders to the storage tank producers, asking them to ensure production and deliver on time, so that they have no capacity to take care of other customers, including Benson.

Without storage tanks, oil producers can only dump the crude oil that they produce into the wilderness. Instead of accepting the oil couldn't be shipped, Mr. Benson made a loud complaint. At the same time, I drastically reduced the price of pipeline transportation, attracted a large amount of oil refiners who rely on Benson to transport crude oil, and converted them to our customers. Before that, I had already quickly acquired several refineries in New York to prevent them from becoming a customer of Benson's.

An excellent commander will not attack a bunker that has nothing to do with him but will try his best to destroy the bunker that is strong enough to destroy the city. Every round of my attack hit places where Mr. Benson had no fuel, and I became the winner. In less than a year after the completion of the longest pipeline, Mr. Benson surrendered. He offered to make peace with me. I know this is not their original intention, but they are well aware that if they continue to fight against me, those who support them will only lose even more.

John, every crucial competition is a battle that determines fate. "Retreat means surrender! Retreat will turn you into a slave!" The war is inevitable, let it come! In this world, competition will not stop for a moment, and we will have no time to rest. All we can do is bring a steel-like determination to face all kinds of challenges and competitions, and we must be in high spirits and happy, otherwise, it will not produce good results.

To win the competition, it is more important that you stay alert. When you constantly see your opponent wanting to weaken you, that is the beginning of the competition. At this point in time you need to know what you have, that kindness and tenderness may hurt you, but then you need to use all the resources to win the battle.

Of course, to win the competition, courage is only one aspect of winning, and you also need to have strength. Crutches cannot replace strong and powerful feet. We must stand on our own feet and rely on ourselves. If your feet are not strong enough to support you, you should not give up and admit defeat, but should work hard to hone, strengthen and develop your feet and let them exert their power.

I think Mr. Benson who is in heaven will agree with me.

Love,
Your Father

LETTER

6

Mortgage for the Future
Borrowing money is to create good luck.

Whether it is to win wealth or to win in life, what good people think when facing competition is not what I will lose, but what I should do to be a winner.

(We are continually faced by greater opportunities brilliantly disguised as insoluble problems)

April 18, 1899

Dear John:

I can understand why using my money to go to the stock market makes you feel a little uneasy. Because you want to win, but you are afraid to lose in that adventurous world, and the lost money is not yours; it is borrowed, and you still have to pay interest.

This kind of unbearable feeling seemed to have been ruling me since the beginning of my entrepreneurship, and even after becoming more accomplished, so every time before borrowing, I will ponder between prudence and adventure, as I struggle, even failing to fall asleep whilst lying on my bed and thinking of ways to repay the debts.

It is often said that people who take risks often fail. But why doesn't this apply to idiots? After my fear of failure, I still managed to always get up and decide to borrow money again. In fact, in order to improve I have no other ways to go, but to borrow from the bank.

Son, what is presented to us is often a great opportunity to solve tricky problems ingeniously. Borrowing money is not a bad thing, it won't make you bankrupt, as long as you don't treat it like a life buoy when you only use it in times of crisis, but instead treat it as a powerful tool, you can use it to create opportunities. Otherwise, you will fall into the quagmire of fear and failure, where fear will restrain you from attaining great achievements, and no success will be achieved in the end.

Among the wealthy people I know or acquainted, there are very few people who rely on accumulating small bits of wealth day by day to eventually become who they are now. More people make money by borrowing money. The reason is not esoteric. Buying and selling a dollar profit each is far less profitable than buying and selling a hundred dollars.

Whether it is to win wealth or to win in life, what good people think about in competition is not what they will lose, but what they should do to become a winner.

Borrowing money is to create good luck. If I can borrow enough cash to mortgage a piece of land and allow myself to monopolize a larger area, then I will seize this opportunity without hesitation. When I was in Cleveland, I won the top position in the Cleveland oil refining industry for expansion. I owed many huge debts, and even mortgaged my business. In the end, I succeeded and created shocking achievements.

Son, life is a constant mortgage, we mortgage our youth for the future, and mortgage our lives for happiness. Because if you dare not approach the bottom line, you lose. Wouldn't it be worthwhile to take the risk to attain success?

When it comes to mortgages, I want to tell you that when I received a huge sum of money from a banker, not only was my business mortgaged, but also my honesty. I regard contracts and contracts as sacred things. I strictly abide by the contracts and never default on debts. I never forget to treat investors, bankers, customers, including competitors with sincerity. When discussing issues with them, I always insist on telling the truth, never making things up or speaking ambiguously, as I firmly believe that lies will always eventually surface.

The rewards of being honest are enormous. Before I walked out of Cleveland, the bankers who knew my character had rescued me from numerous crises that were hard to escape from.

I clearly remember that one day, one of my oil refineries suddenly caught fire and I suffered heavy losses. Since the insurance company was unable to pay the insurance premium, and I needed a sum of money to rebuild the enterprise. I had to make additional loans to the bank. Now the thought of the bank loan that day made me excited. Originally, in the eyes of the bankers who lacked vision, the oil refining industry was already a high-risk industry. Providing funds to this industry was no less than gambling, plus my oil refinery was just destroyed, so some bank directors were hesitant on the additional loan and did not approve them.

At this moment, one kind soul, Mr. Stillman, asked a staff member to bring his own safe and waved at several other directors: "Listen to me, gentlemen, Mr. Rockefeller and his partners are very well accomplished people. If they want to lend more money, I urge you to lend them without hesitation. If you want to be more assured, take however much you need." I subdued the bankers with my honesty.

Son, honesty is a method and a strategy. Because I paid with my own honesty, I have won the trust of bankers and more people, and because of it I survived numerous difficult times, and embarked on an expressway to success.

Today, I no longer need to turn to any bank. I am my own bank, but I will always be grateful to the bankers who have helped me so much.

Your future may be managing a business. You need to know that the purpose of running a business is to make money. Expanding an enterprise can make money but mortgaging a company is also an important matter with regards to managing and using money. If you only focus on one function and ignore the other, you will face failure; in the worst case, it may cause a financial collapse, and in a better case, you may miss many opportunities.

Managing and using money is different from the determination to make money and it requires different beliefs. To manage and use money, you must be willing to manage the numbers yourself, and not just simply talk about management and strategy. God is shown in the details. If you neglect these details, or detach from the details, and authorize this "miscellaneous task" to others to do, it is equivalent to neglecting at least half of your important business responsibility. The details should never hinder enthusiasm. To be successful you need to remember two things: one is tactics and the other is strategy.

Son, you are moving towards winning a great life. This has been your goal all the time. You need to be brave and do so continually.

Love,
Your Father

LETTER

7

The most horrifying thing is Spiritual Bankruptcy
Failure is a good thing as long as it does not become a habit.

When you take advantage of opportunities, you are depriving others of opportunities in order to guarantee yourself.

Once avoiding failure becomes your motivation to do things, you have embarked on a path of laziness and powerlessness.

(An optimist sees an opportunity in every calamity, a pessimist sees a calamity in every opportunity.)

November 19, 1899

Dear John:

Your mood has been very down lately, which makes me sad. I can really feel that you are still ashamed and humiliated from the investment that cost you a million dollars. This caused you to feel depressed and worried all day long. However, this is not necessary, a failure does not show anything, and will not put the label of incompetency on your forehead.

Be happy, my son. You need to know that no one in this world leads a smooth life; on the contrary, they live side by side with failure. Perhaps it is because there are so many helpless failures in this world that the pursuit of excellence becomes fascinating that it still makes people chase after it, even at the expense of their life. Even so, failure still comes.

Our fate is the same. It is just that unlike some people, I take failure as a glass of spirits. It is bitter when you drink it, yet it gives you plenty of vitality.

When I first stepped into the business world and prayed to the God to bless our new company, a catastrophic storm hit us. At that time, we signed a contract to buy a large amount of beans and were prepared to make a lot of money, but we did not expect that a sudden "visit" from frost would come and crush our sweet dreams. Half of the beans we got were destroyed, and some unscrupulous suppliers also added sand, small beans, and straw. This business was destined to fail. But I know that I cannot be depressed, let alone be immersed in failure, otherwise, I will drift further away from my goals and dreams.

There is no free lunch in the world, and it is even more impossible to maintain the status quo. If you stay still, you will regress, but to move forward you must be willing to make decisions and take risks. After that business failed, I borrowed money from my father again, although I was not very reluctant to do so. Moreover, to make myself superior in managing my business, I told my partner Mr. Clark that we must promote ourselves and let our potential customers know through newspaper advertisements that we can provide large prepayments and can supply large amounts of agricultural products in advance.

As a result, courage and diligence saved us. In that year, instead of being affected by the "bean incident", we made a considerable net profit.

Everyone hates failure. However, once avoiding failure becomes your motivation for doing things, you embark on a path of laziness and powerlessness. This is terrible, especially for such a disaster. Because this heralds the possibility that people might lose the opportunities they might have.

Son, opportunity is a scarce thing. People are prosperous and rich because of opportunity. Look at those poor people and you will know that they are not incompetent or stupid neither are they not hard-working. They are deprived from opportunities. You need to know that we live in a jungle where the weak are prey to the strong, where you either eat people or risk being eaten by someone else. Evading risk is almost a guarantee of bankruptcy; but when you take advantage of the opportunity, you are depriving others of the opportunity just to guarantee yourself.

If you are afraid of failure, you will not dare to take risks and then lose the opportunities that are placed right in front of you. Therefore, my son, in order to avoid losing opportunities and retain your qualifications for competition, it is worthwhile to pay for our failures and setbacks!

Failure is the beginning of the journey to a higher position. I can say that what I have achieved today was from climbing the spiral ladder of failure and then rose from there. I am a clever "loser". I know to learn from failures, draw success factors from my experience thru failure, and use innovative methods that I have never thought of before to start a new career. So, I want to say that failure is a good thing as long as it does not become a habit.

My motto is: People always have to maintain their energy, remain strong and persistent, no matter what failures and setbacks they encounter, this is the only thing I can do. I myself can understand what I should do to make myself feel happy, and what is worth my efforts. Fundamental expectations, like a broom in the hands of a cleaner, will sweep away all the trash that you face when on your way to success. Son, what are your fundamental expectations? As long as you don't throw it away, success will surely come.

Optimistic people will see opportunity in suffering, and pessimistic people will see suffering in opportunity. Son, remember the formula of success that I believe in:

Dream + Failure + Challenge = Success

Of course, failure has its lethal power, it can make people depressed, decadent, lose their fighting spirit and willpower. What matters is what you see failure as. The genius inventor Mr. Thomas Edison, before illuminating Mr. Morgan's office with electric lights, conducted a total of more than 10,000 experiments. To him, failure is a test field for success.

Ten years ago, a young reporter from The New York Sun interviewed him, and asked: "Mr. Edison, your current invention has failed 10,000 times. What do you think of this?" Edison was very immune to the word failure. He said to the reporter in a wise manner: "Young man, your journey of life has just begun, so I tell you that will help you a lot in the future. I have not failed 10,000 times, I just invented 10,000 unworkable methods." The power of spirit is always so great.

Son, if you declare spiritual/mental bankruptcy, you will lose everything. You need to know that the career path is like a wave. If you step on the wave, the merits will follow; and if you make a mistake, you will be trapped in the shallows and sorrow for the rest of your life. Failure is a learning experience. You can either turn it into a tombstone or a steppingstone.

There is no success without challenges. Do not stop because of a failure and overcome yourself. You are the biggest winner!

I have great faith in you.

Love,
Your Father

LETTER

8

Only giving up will result in failure

There is nothing in the world that can replace perseverance.

Unless you give up, you will not be beaten.

Too many people overestimate what they lack, but underestimate what they have.

(Too many people overvalue what they are not and undervalue what they are.)

February 12, 1909

Dear John:

Today is a great day!

Today, the United States cherish a peculiar feeling of gratitude to commemorate the great and rare soul – the former president, Mr. Abraham Lincoln, who is worthy of God and mankind. I believe Lincoln deserves it.

In my real memory, no one is greater than Lincoln. He has woven a successful and moving history of the United States. With his indomitable spirit, courage, and generosity, he liberated four million of the humblest black slaves and crushed 27 million locks that have been placed on the soul of people of colour. This put an end to the sinful history of depraved, twisted, and narrow souls due to racial hatred. He avoided the disaster of the country's destruction and combined all different languages, religions, skin colours, and races into a brand-new country. The United States became free because of him, and fortunately embarked on the broad road of integrity and justice.

Lincoln was the greatest hero of the last century. Today, on this occasion of his centennial birthday, the whole country remembers what he has done for the United States, which is the best proof.

However, when we reappear and appreciate his glorious cause, we should absorb and expand the special lessons of his life-persistent determination and courage. I think the best way for us to commemorate him is to imitate him and let his spirit of perseverance illuminate America.

In my heart, Lincoln will always be the indomitable embodiment who is not frightened by difficulties. He was born impoverished and was driven out of his home. He failed on his first time in business, and the second time he failed even worse, so it took him more than ten years to pay off his debts. His road to politics was similarly bumpy. He lost his first campaign for state and lost his job. Fortunately, his second campaign was successful. But what followed was the loss of a loved one, and failure to be elected as the state senator spokesperson. However, he was not discouraged. In the subsequent elections, he failed six times, but even after each defeat, he was still striving for the top, until he was elected as the President of the United States.

Everyone has gone through the vicissitudes of life and suffered mercilessly, but only a few people can be as resilient as Lincoln. After every failed campaign Lincoln would motivate himself: "This is just a slip up, not as if I'm dead and unable to get up." These words held the power to overcome difficulties, and they were also the weapon that led Lincoln to fame.

Lincoln's life wrote a great truth: unless you give up, you will not be defeated.

Success is a series of struggles. Almost all those great figures have suffered a series of merciless blows. Each of them almost surrendered, but they finally achieved brilliant results because of their persistence. For example, the great Greek orator Demosthenes, he was shy because he stuttered. After his father died, he left him a piece of land in hopes that he could live a prosperous life. However, the Greek law at the time stipulated that he must win the ownership of the land by debating in public before declaring his right to own the land. Unfortunately, because of his stuttering and shyness, he suffered a fiasco, and as a result he lost that piece of land. But he was not knocked down, instead he worked hard to better himself. As a result, he created an unprecedented speech climax. History has overlooked the man who acquired his property, but for centuries, the whole of Europe has remembered a great name— Demosthenes.

Too many people overestimate what they lack, but underestimate what they have, and lose the chance to become a winner. This is a tragedy.

Lincoln's life is a great testimony of turning setbacks into victory. There is no lucky person who does not fail. It is important not to become a coward because of failure. If we do our best and still fail to achieve the goal, all we should do is to learn our lesson and strive to perform better next time.

Frankly speaking, I have no intention to compare with President Lincoln, but I have some of his spirit. I hate it when my business fails and lose money, but what really concerns me is that I am afraid that in future business, I will be too cautious and become a coward. If that is the case, then my loss will be even greater.

For ordinary people, failure is difficult to keep them on, while success is easy to continue. But this is an exception for Lincoln, for he will use all kinds of frustration and failure to drive him to the next level. Because he has steel-like perseverance. He has a saying which was said well: "You can't sharpen your razor on a velvet."

There is nothing in the world that can replace perseverance. Talent is not acceptable. Unprecedented talents abound, and geniuses who accomplish nothing is common; education is also not acceptable. The world is full of people who are useless in learning. Only perseverance and determination will never be disadvantageous.

As we continue to reach the peak, we must remember: each step of the ladder allows us enough time to step on, and then set foot to a higher level, it is not for us to rest. We are tired and discouraged on the way, but like a boxer said, you must fight another round to win. When encountering difficulties, we must fight another round. Everyone has unlimited potential inside, and unless we know where it is and insist on using it, it is worthless.

Great opportunities do not seek external validation; however, we must work hard to grasp them. As the saying goes: "Strike while the iron's hot." It's really good. Perseverance and hard work are both important. Every "no" brings us closer and closer to a "yes". "Before dawn is always the darkest", this sentence is not a catchphrase. When we work hard and make use of our skills, a successful day will eventually come.

Today, as we are grateful and praise President Lincoln, we must not forget to use his life's deeds to inspire ourselves. Even if we do so, our indomitable day has yet to come, and we are still a big winner. Because we already have knowledge and know how to face life, that is greater success.

Love,
Your Father

LETTER

9

Faith is Gold

The level of confidence determines the level of achievement.

As long as we believe that we can succeed, we will succeed.

I never believed that failure is the mother of success, I believe that faith is the father of success.

(The force which have lighted my way, and time after time have given me new courage to face life cheerfully, have been confidence.)

June 7, 1903

Dear John:

You are right, the wisdom of a talented person can create miracles. However, the reality is that there are always very few people who create miracles, but there are many ordinary people who emerge.

Intriguingly, everyone wants to do a lot. Everyone wants to get some of the best things. Everyone does not like to fawn on others and lead a mediocre life, and no one likes to think that he/she is a second-tier person or feel that he is forced into this situation.

Is this because we don't have the general wisdom of talents? No! The most practical wisdom for success has long been written in the "Bible", that is, "Unshakable faith is enough to move mountains." But why are there so many losers? I think that is because there are not many people who truly believe that they can move out. As a result, not many people really can.

Most people regard that holy word as an absurd idea, thinking that it is simply impossible. I think these people who cannot be saved have made a common-sense mistake. They mistook *faith* for *hope*. It is true that we cannot use *hope* to move a mountain, cannot rely on *hope* to win victory or make progress, nor can we rely on *hope* to have wealth and status.

However, the power of *faith* can help us move a mountain. In other words, as long as we believe we can succeed. You may think that I am miraculous or mystifying the power of *faith*, no! Confidence produces the attitude of believing in "I can do it", and the attitude of believing in "I can do it" can produce the abilities, skills, and energy. Whenever you believe that "I can do it", you will naturally come up with a "how to solve" method, and success is born once you successfully solve the problem. This is the process of confidence displaying its might.

Everyone *hopes* that one day they can reach the highest level and enjoy the fruits of success that follows. However, most of them do not have the required confidence and determination, hence they cannot reach the top. It is also because they believe that they cannot reach it, so they find a route to take where they cannot reach the top, and their actions always stay at the level of ordinary people.

However, a few of my friends really believe that they will succeed one day. They carry out various tasks with the mentality of "I'm going to the top" and achieve their goals with strong confidence. I thought I was one of them. When I was a poor boy, I was confident that I would become the richest person in the world. Strong self-confidence inspired me to come up with various feasible plans, methods, means and techniques, and one step at a time to climb to the top of the oil kingdom.

I never believed that failure is the mother of success, I believe that faith is the father of success. Victory is a habit, and failure is also a habit. If you want to succeed, you must achieve sustained victory. I do not like to achieve a certain amount of victory. What I want is sustained victory. Only in this way can I become a strong one. Confidence motivates me to succeed.

Believing that there will be great results is the driving force behind all great careers, books, scripts, and new scientific knowledge. Believing in success is a basic and absolutely necessary element possessed by successful people. But the loser has graciously discarded these.

I have talked to many people who have failed in their business and have heard countless reasons and excuses for failure. When these losers were speaking, they would often unwittingly say: "To be honest, I didn't think it would work." "I felt uneasy before I started." "In fact, it's not too surprising that this has failed."

Adopting an attitude of "I will give it a try, but I don't think there will be any results" will lead to failure in the end. "Disbelief" is a negative force. When you disagree or have doubts in your mind, you will come up with various reasons to support your "disbelief". Suspicion, disbelief, the tendency to fail subconsciously, and the lack of desire to succeed are the main causes of failure. If you doubt it, you will fail. If you believe in victory, you will definitely succeed.

The level of confidence determines the level of achievement. Mediocre people who live their life day by day believing that they can't do anything, will only get a small amount of numeration. They believe that they cannot do great things, so they really could not. They think that they are very unimportant, and everything they do is insignificant. Over time, even their words and actions will show a lack of self-confidence. If they cannot raise their self-confidence, they will shrink in their self-judgements and become increasingly insignificant. And what they think of themselves will also make others think of them in the same manner, so these kinds of people will become insignificant in the eyes of everyone.

Those who move forward, and affirm that they have greater value, will get high rewards. He believes that he can handle difficult tasks and can really do it. Everything he does, his dealings with others, his personality, thoughts and opinions all shows that he is an expert and also an indispensable and important person.

It is faith that illuminates my path, constantly gives me courage, and makes me face life positively. At any time, I never forget to increase my confidence. I replace the thought of failure with the belief of success. When I face a difficult situation, I think of "I will win" instead of "I might lose". When I compete with people, I think of "I am as good as them", not "I can't compare with them." When opportunities arise, I think of "I can do it" instead of "I can't do it."

Everyone's first step towards success, and also the basic step that cannot be missed, is to believe in yourself and believe that you will be able to succeed. Let the key idea "I will succeed" dominate our various thinking processes. The belief in success will inspire my faith in creating plans for success. The idea of failure is just the opposite, as it makes us think about some ideas that will lead to failure.

I remind myself regularly: You are better than you think. Successful people are not supermen. Success does not require superhuman intelligence, it is not about luck, and there is no mystery. Successful people are just ordinary people who believe in themselves and affirm what they do. Never, never sell yourself cheaply.

Everyone is a product of his thoughts, thinking about small goals, will lead to small results. Thinking of great goals will win great success. And great ideas and big plans usually come easier than small ones, at least it will not be more difficult.

Those who can reach the pinnacle in business, mission, writing, acting, and other pursuits of achievement are all because they can steadily and persistently pursue a plan of self-development and growth. This training program will bring them a series of rewards: getting more respected by their family members; getting praises from friends and colleagues; rewards that feel useful to them; rewards for becoming important people; increasing income and renumeration which improves their living standards.

Success – achievement – is the ultimate goal in life. She needs to cherish my credible and active thinking. Of course, I do not think I can let my beliefs go wrong at any time.

Love,
Your Father

LETTER

10

Loyal to oneself

I can deceive the enemy, but I will never deceive myself.

People who ask me to treat them with sincerity want to reap benefits from me.

What fate gives us is not the wine of disappointment, but the cup of opportunity.

(Our destiny offers not the cup of despair, but the chalice of opportunity.)

November 29, 1899

Dear John:

Are you in a better mood? If not, I think, you need to know something.

You need to know that in this world, the vast majority of people are not immune to a special force that can easily peel off the cloak that wraps our humanity, and expose us completely to the sun and justly delineates us on the pure and dirty plates, so that all our defenses become pale and weak. No matter how clever we are, it is the test of our humanity: interest/benefits.

In other words, interest is the shadow that illuminates human nature. In front of it, all the essences related to morality and ethics will be revealed and unobstructed. Maybe you think my words are a little absolute, but this is what my experience tells me.

I am not a human historian. I don't know what explanation they will give to explain the nobility and ugliness of people, but my life course makes me firmly believe that interests seem to be invincible, and It can bring people, races, and countries who could have lived peacefully with one another together, and make people deceive each other. In those scams, traps of defamation, slander, and vilification, as well as cruel and merciless bloody battles and robber-style plunder, you will find the shadows that are chasing interests. In this sense, it is more accurate to say that we are slaves of interest rather than masters of our own souls.

I can assert that in this world, apart from God, there is no one who does not pursue profit. From the moment you step into interpersonal relationships, a protracted life game for profit begins. In this game, everyone is your enemy, including yourself. You need to fight against your weaknesses and against all the evils that build happiness on your pain. Therefore, when I saw through all this, I always adhered to a principle: I can deceive the enemy, but I never deceive myself. Fighting back at the enemy who is shooting me will never disturb my conscience.

Son, please don't get me wrong, I don't intend to paint our world with an oppressive and suffocating grey; in fact, I long for friendship, sincerity, kindness and all the beautiful emotions that can nourish my soul, and I believe in them. It must exist. However, it is a pity that in the market of chasing fame and fortune, it is difficult for me to get this kind of satisfaction, and I often encounter betrayal and deception. To this day, I can still clearly remember the experiences of being deceived several times, which is unforgettable.

The most painful deceit I experienced occurred in Cleveland. At that time, the oil refining industry was almost unprofitable due to overproduction, and many oil refiners had fallen into bankruptcy. Also, Cleveland is far away from the oil field, which means that compared with those refineries in the oil field, we had to pay a premium for the long-distance transportation which put ourselves in an unfair position. I am determined to change it. I want to acquire a large-scale refinery that is struggling on the death line, forming a joint force and a unified action, so that everyone's wallet will bulge.

I told those refinery owners who were on the verge of bankruptcy that "we are at a disadvantage in Cleveland and what we must do to protect ourselves together. I think my plan is very good, please think about it. If you are interested, we will be happy to discuss with you." Because of my kind wishes and strategic considerations, I bought many worthless factories. They are just like old rubbish, only worth throwing into the scrap iron pile.

But some people are so evil, selfish, and ungrateful. After they got my money, they became enemies, unscrupulously tore up their agreement with me, made a comeback, bought equipment with money earned with my help, returned to their old business, and publicly blackmailed me, asking me to buy their factory. These people have asked me to be honest and buy their paralyzed factory. I did it. However, the results were distressing. At that moment, my mood was terrible, and I even blamed myself for being honest and kind, otherwise I would not be embarrassed and helpless.

What is the most unacceptable is that in profit-making games, today's friends will become tomorrow's enemies. This situation often happens, and my two church members have deceived me many times without restraining. For the sake of God, I do not want to count their sins. But I can tell you, I was shocked when I knew that I had been deceived by them. I do not understand why people who pray with me and swear religiously will want to abandon their pride, indulgence and greed, how can they be so despicable!

After all kinds of deceptions and lies, I told myself helplessly: You can only believe in yourself, and only in this way, you will not be deceived. I know this kind of slightly hostile mentality is not good, but there are too many deceptions in this world, and guarding ourselves is an indispensable survival skill.

Dealing with bastards will make you smart. Those evil "teachers" taught me a lot. If anyone wants to deceive me now, I guess it will be more difficult than crossing the Grand Canyon, because those demons helped me establish a set of rules for dealing with people, I think this set of rules will help you:

I only show my feelings when the situation is only beneficial to myself; I can let my opponent teach me, but I will never teach my opponent, no matter how much I know about it; think twice about everything, no matter how others may urge, do not act without making a full consideration; I have my own truth, only responsible for myself; be careful of those who ask me to treat them sincerely, they want to reap benefits from me.

I know that deception is only a strategy in a profit-making game and cannot solve the problem. But I also know that games for profit are played day and night, so I must be vigilant from morning to night and understand: in this game, everyone is the enemy, because everyone takes care of their own interests first, whether or not it is good for others. The important thing is knowing how to protect yourself and prepare for war anytime, anywhere.

Son, what destiny gives us is not the wine of disappointment, but the cup of opportunity, cheer up! What happened on Wall Street is nothing special, it is just that you believe in others too much. However, you need to know that a good horse will not fall twice in the same place.

Love,
Your Father

LETTER

11

Greed is necessary
Let every thought be subjected to profitable motives.

I am the focus of my life; I decide what suits me.

Destiny must be created by oneself, and what you really want must be obtained by every means.

(Simplicity is an uptightness of soul that has no reference to self; it is different from sincerity, and it is a still higher virtue.)

May 6, 1918

Dear John:

Ignore those who say I am greedy.

For many years, I have been enjoying this "praise" that seems not so wonderful to others – Greed. This special tribute to me first appeared when my career was in full swing, when Rockefeller's name was no longer just a symbol of a person, but a symbol of wealth, and a huge business empire.

I remember that many people and many newspapers joined the ranks of "praising" me. But this kind of praise did not make my heart beat faster, even though I know that it is nothing more than to discredit me, and it is nothing more than to add a filthy lucre to the business empire I have created.

But I know that there is a kind of power hidden in human nature, one that grows in places lacking ability and will, that is jealousy. When you surpass them, they will hate you, accuse you using derogatory words, fabricate lies to slander you, and at the same time they will be very arrogant in front of you – in my opinion, that is not arrogance, it is just weakness. What's interesting is that when you are far inferior to them, and your life is unbearable, they will laugh at you again, for being incompetent, stupid, and even belittle you to the point that you have no human dignity. My son, this is human nature!

God did not give me a mission to change human nature, and I did not take the time to stop those people from wanting to "praise" me for being greedy. All I can do is to keep those who are jealous of me jealous! Although, I know that if I let them take away all the wealth that I have created, they will also take away their praise for me, but I can't! I believe that unless there is some magic, no one can!

A gentleman will never argue with the ignorant, and I certainly will not argue with those who "praised" my greed, but I cannot refrain from despising their ignorance. Looking back calmly at history and examining the footprints of mankind, we can conclude that no society is not built on greed. Those who want to slander me, seemingly as if they are moral watchmen, which one of them would not want to monopolize what they have? Who does not want to control all the good things? Who does not want to control everything that everyone needs? There are always many hypocritical people.

There is no one who is not greedy. If you have an olive, you will want to have an entire olive tree. I have been living in the world for nearly 80 years. I have seen people who cannot eat steak, but I have never seen anyone who is not greedy, especially in the business world. There is only one word printed on the back of utilitarianism and money worship, that is greed. I believe that people who are not greedy in the future will still be rare on earth. Who will stop the pursuit and possession of beautiful things?

Mr. Archibald said that I am a racehorse that could smell the finish line, but as soon as that happened, I would start sprinting. I know this is a bit flattering, but in my heart, I really reserved a place for greed.

When I was in business school, one of my teachers said a phrase that I will never forget. It can be said to have changed my destiny. He said: "There is nothing wrong with being greedy. I think being greedy is a good thing. Everyone can be greedy. From the beginning of greed, there will be hope!"

When my teacher shouted this extremely provocative and irritating remark from the forum, the students in the audience were in an uproar. As long as you think about the meaning of "greedy", you will know that this word completely violates the moral concept that most people have learned since childhood. This moral concept is integrated into religion, society, ethics, politics, and law. The role of a ruler will undoubtedly put a dirty mark on this word.

But when I stepped into the society and embarked on the journey of creating wealth, I deeply realized that the classes I took was really worth it. My teacher's proposition was quite insightful. As those evolutionists told us, nature is not a benevolent and selfless place, but a place where the strong are kings and the fittest live, so is our so-called civilized society. If you are not greedy, you may just be "eaten" by others. After all, there are not many delicious desserts.

If you want to create wealth and achievements, and an extraordinary life, then I feel that you can forget about "greed is a good thing", greed is necessary!

The subtext of greed is that, I want more, and monopolize it! Who has never made this cry in my heart? Politicians will say, I want to be in power, and I want to be the governor before being the president. Businesspeople will say, I want to make money, I want to make more money. Parents will say that I hope my son can achieve something and live a prosperous and happy life forever. And so on. Only when limited by morality, dignity, and face value, can people tightly cover up greed and make greed a taboo.

In fact, as long as the world that wants to chase fame and fortune is not destroyed, as long as happiness does not become as easy to get as air, human beings cannot stop being greedy.

Those who love muckraking always regard greed as a demon. But in my opinion, opening the lock of our greed is not the same as opening the Pandora's Box, and releasing the beating greed all the time is equivalent to releasing the potential of our lives. From a bookkeeper with a weekly salary of only five dollars to the richest person in the United States today, it was greed which made me achieve this miracle. Greed is the force that drives me to create wealth, just as it is the force that drives social evolution.

When I use the word greed, you might want me to replace it with aspiration. No, we are all in a greedy world. I think using greed is simpler than using ambition. Simplicity is a quality of integrity and selflessness in the soul. It is different and more noble than sincerity.

At the beginning of co-founding the oil company with Mr. Sam Andrews, my greed was swelling. Every night before going to bed, I advised myself: I want to become the largest oil refiner in Cleveland, let the flowing oil creek turn into bundles of banknotes, I want to align every thought to profit motives and help myself become the king of oil. In the early days, I would do everything by myself and work all day long. I direct oil refining, organize railway transportation, and contemplate how to save costs and expand the petroleum by-product market. I will never forget the days that left me starving and rushing around day and night.

My son, destiny must be created by oneself, and what one really wants must be obtained by every means. The distance between success and failure is not just a single thought as what people may think, that is to see who has the stronger greed, who has this power, who can radiate and display all their power, do their best, and surpass themselves. Every step I move forward can make me feel the power of greed! Greed not only allows a person's abilities to be maximized, but also forces him to dedicate everything, remove all obstacles, and move forward at full speed.

Many people have asked me the same question: "Mr. Rockefeller, what supported you on your way to the top of wealth?" I cannot express my true feelings because greed is despised by people. However, the fact is that greed is the support that supported me to become a generation of millionaire, that is, I aroused my greed and deepened my greed.

There is a lively, sensitive, and powerful greed in everyone's heart. But you must love her, tell yourself that you want to be greedy, and you want more, then she will come out to play and help you succeed.

No force can stop me from lifting the ban on greed because I pursue success. Success achieved under greed is not a sin. Success is a noble pursuit. If you can achieve success with noble behaviour, you will contribute far more to mankind than what can be done in poverty. I did it!

Let us look at the philanthropies we have done today. Investing huge wealth in education, medicine, churches, and those in need is definitely not a place for me to do charity on a whim. It is a great charity, and the world is becoming more beautiful because of my success. It seems that greed is very good, and not a crime.

In this regard, if those who say I am greedy are not for the purpose of discrediting me, I will gladly accept the judgment they make of me.

John, I am the focus of my life, I decide what suits me, so I do not care what those people say, my heart is still peaceful. To some people, I always seem to be a businessman with despicable motives. Even if I invest in charities that benefit the people, It will be regarded as a trick by them. They suspect that the motivation of my charities is to pursue self-interest, or a form of atoning my sins, but they do not see it as a selfless spirit of public welfare. This is really funny.

I want to tell you very sincerely that your father will never make you feel ashamed. Every penny in my pocket is clean. The reason why I became rich is my superior mind and strong career. The heart is rewarded. I firmly believe that God has clear rewards and punishments, and that my money is given by God. And I can always make money. If God helps, this is because God knows that I will return the money to society for the benefit of my fellow citizens.

It is time for me to read the Bible. The night is so beautiful tonight, every bright star seems to say: "Good job! John."

Love,
Your Father

LETTER

12

Hell is full of good people
Arrogance usually leads to downfall.

I do not like money, what I like is making money.

My belief is to reach the goal before others.

(The people who get on in the world are the people who look for the circumstances they want, if they cannot find them, make them.)

August 11, 1918

Dear John:

Today, on my way to play golf, I encountered a challenge that I have not met in a long time: a young man arrogantly overtook my car in his fashionable Chevrolet. He provoked this old man's competitive nature, and in the end, he could only look at the back of my car. This made me very happy, just like when I defeated my opponent in the business.

John, eagerness is my nature that never wears off, so I say that those who condemn my endless greed are wrong. In fact, I do not like money. What I like is making money. What I like is the good feeling of victory.

Of course, the feeling when others lose sometimes touches my compassion, but doing business is a harsh competition. There is nothing more ruthless than the determination to force others out, but you can only avoid the tragic fate of defeat by finding ways to defeat your opponent. This is the case when there is competition.

It is undeniable that if you want to succeed, you often must sacrifice others. However, if you pursue victory and hope to win, you must resist the idea of sympathizing with others. You cannot just want to be a good person, you can't retain your strength, you can't evade or delay letting your opponent out. You know, hell is full of good people, and the pain of failure is part of the business war. We are all strangling our opponents. Without the determination to compete and fight to the end, we only have the qualifications to be losers.

Frankly speaking, I do not like competition, but I try to compete. Whenever I encounter a strong opponent, the competitiveness in my heart will burn, and when it extinguishes, what I gain is victory and happiness. Mr. Potts once brought me this kind of pleasure, and he was great.

The war with Mr. Potts was due to a mistake of mine, a mistake made out of kindness. In the 1870s, oil was concentrated in a small area in north-western Pennsylvania. If an oil pipeline network was built there to connect all the oil wells, I only needed one valve to control the entire oil region. Thus, completely dominating the industry. But I am worried that using pipelines for long-distance transportation will cause anxiety and fear to the railway companies that I work with. Therefore, in order to protect their interests, I did not launch any plans to lay oil pipelines, especially because they have helped me before.

However, the Pennsylvania Railroad Company, which had tricked yet still made compromises with me, was ambitious. They tried to replace me and put the oil refining industry under their control. They merged the two largest oil pipelines in the oil area into their own railway network to get our necks stuck. And the person responsible for accomplishing this mission is Mr. Potts, president of Empire Transportation Company, a subsidiary of Pennsylvania Railroad Company.

Sitting and watching the opponent, even if the strength of the potential opponent increases, it will weaken one's own strength and even subvert one's position. I am not that stupid. My belief is to reach the goal before others. I quickly set up the U.S. Transportation Company with the shrewd and capable Mr. Odai and launched a self-defence counterattack with the Empire Transportation Company. Thank God, our efforts paid off. Within a year, we controlled 40% of the oil transportation business in the oil region and suppressed Mr. Potts' attack. But this is just the beginning of my contest with Mr. Potts.

The people who can get ahead in this world are those who know how to find their ideal environment. If they cannot do it, they will create it themselves.

Two years later, a new oil field was discovered in Bradford, Pennsylvania. Mr. Odai quickly led his people to the place that aroused the dream of millions of people to make a fortune and paved the oil pipeline to the new oil well day and night. But all the guys in the oil field were crazy and unrestrained. They could not wait to collect all the oil overnight, and then left with joy on their faces. Therefore, no matter how hard Mr. Odai and others worked, they cannot meet the needs of transportation and storage of oil.

I do not want to see the hard-working oil producers dig their own graves and destroy themselves. I asked Mr. Odai to warn oil producers that their extraction capacity had far exceeded our transportation capacity. They must reduce production, otherwise the black gold that comes out will become worthless black soil. But no one accepted our kindness and advice, and no one appreciated our efforts, and instead denounced us, saying that we did not want to procure their oil.

Just as when the oil producers in Bradford were at the peak of their emotions, Mr. Potts started taking action. He first led a series of demonstration at our oil refineries in New York, Philadelphia, and Pittsburgh to acquire our competitor's refineries; then, he began to seize the site in Bradford and laid oil pipelines to transport Bradford's crude oil to his own refinery.

I admired Mr. Potts' courage and I was more than willing to accept the challenge he sought to shake my dominance in the oil refining industry, but I must drive him out of the oil refining industry.

I first met up with the owner of Pennsylvania Railroad Company, Mr. Scott. I told him bluntly that Mr. Potts was a poacher and he was breaking into our territory. We must stop him. But Mr. Scott was very stubborn and determined to allow Potts' thieving to continue. I had no choice but to challenge this powerful enemy.

First, we terminated all business dealings with Pennsylvania Railroad Company. I instructed our subordinates to transfer the transportation business to the two major railway companies that have always firmly supported us, asked them to reduce freight rates, compete with Pennsylvania Railroad Company, weaken its power; and at the same time order all refineries in Pittsburgh that depend on the Empire Company for transportation to close; subsequently they instructed all its own refineries that were in competition with the Empire Company to sell refined oil at prices far lower than them. Pennsylvania Railroad Company is the largest transportation company in the United States. Mr. Scott held large power when it comes to transportation. They were proud that they have never been conquered. But under my three-dimensional oppressive style of play, they could only surrender.

To fight against me, they reluctantly gave our competitors huge discounts. In other words, they paid others even when serving them. Then they resorted to an unpopular move – cutting employee and cutting wages. Scott and Potts did not expect that this would soon lead to punishment. In order to vent their dissatisfaction, the angry workers burned hundreds of tankers and locomotives in a fire, forcing them to ask the Wall Street Bank for an emergency loan. As a result, not only did the shareholders of Pennsylvania Railroad Company not get any dividends, but the stock price plummeted. As a result of their duel with me, their pockets were getting cleaner.

Mr. Potts is indeed a soldier. In the smoke of life and death, he has spelt out the rank of colonel. He has an admirable and unyielding willpower. Therefore, even after the victor emerged, he still wanted to continue fighting with me. But Mr. Scott, who also has a military career,- and was the most authoritative ruling and powerful figure, knows more about the current affairs. He decisively lowered his arrogance and sent someone to tell me that he hoped to make peace and stop the oil refining business.

I know that Colonel Potts wanted to prove himself to the great Moses, but he failed, he failed completely. A few years later, Potts gave up his desire to confront me and became an active and diligent director of one of my companies. This shrewd and slippery oil dealer!

Arrogance usually leads to downfall. Scott and Potts and his ilk thought they were of noble origin and were always arrogant. Therefore, my heart was fluttering when I successfully tamed these arrogant donkeys.

John, I like victory, but I do not like unscrupulous pursuit of victory. A victory at any cost is not a victory. The ugly means of competition is disgusting. It is tantamount to painting the ground as a prison. You may never be able to surpass it. Even if you win a victory, you may lose the chance to win again.

And compliance does not mean that we must lower our determination to pursue victory, but it means using an ethical way to win a clear victory, and it also means that under such restrictions, we must strive to pursue victory fairly and ruthlessly. I hope you can do this.

Love,
Your Father

LETTER

13

There is no free lunch in the world

If You want to make a person disabled, just give him a pair of crutches.

Deny his dignity, and you take away his fate.

The first and last chapter of the book of wisdom is that there is no free lunch in the world.

(Both within and without, a little of that constitutes the dignity of life and death.)

March 17, 1911

Dear John:

I have noticed the news that accused me of being stingy, saying that I do not donate enough. It is nothing. I have been scolded enough by reporters who do not know me, and I am used to their ignorance and harshness. There is only one way I respond to them: to remain silent and unjustified, no matter how they verbally criticize me. Because I know what I think, I firmly believe that I am on the right side.

Everyone needs to go their own way, and it is important to have a clear conscience. There is a story that may explain why I rarely pay attention to the beggars who beg me to give them money to solve their personal problems, and it can also explain why this makes me more nervous than earning money.

The story goes like this:

There was a farmer who kept a few pigs in captivity. One day, the owner forgot to close the door and gave the pigs a chance to escape. After a few generations, these pigs became more and more fierce and began to threaten pedestrians passing by. Several experienced hunters heard about this and wanted to capture them for the people. However, these pigs were very cunning and could never be fooled.

John, when the pigs start to become independent, they will become tough and smart.

One day, an old man was chasing a donkey that was dragging a two-wheeled cart with a lot of wood and grain when he walked into a village where the "wild boars" roamed. The locals were very curious, so they walked forward and asked the old man: "Where are you from, what are you going to do?" The old man told them, "I'll help you catch the wild boars!" The villagers laughed at him as soon as they heard it: "Don't be funny now, how can you do something that even a good hunter could not do." However, two months later, the old man came back and told the villagers in that village that the wild boars had been locked in a fence on the top of the mountain.

The villagers were surprised again, and asked the old man: "Really? Unbelievable, how did you catch them?" The old man explained, "First of all, go to a place where wild boars often come out to eat. Then, I put some food in the middle of the open space as a bait for the trap. The pigs were startled at first, but eventually ran over curiously to smell the food. Soon an old wild boar ate the first bite, and other wild boars followed. I knew then, I must be able to catch them.

"The next day, I added a little more food and planted a plank a few feet away. The board temporarily frightened them off like a ghost, but the free lunch was tempting, so they soon ran back to continue eating. At the time, the wild boar did not know that they were going to be mine. After that, all I have to do is to plant a few more boards around the grain every day until my trap is complete."

"Then I dug a hole and erected the first corner pile. Every time I add something, they will stay away for some time, but in the end, they will come again for free lunch. The fence is built, and the trap door is ready. Well, the habit of getting something for nothing made them walk into the fence without any hesitation. At this time, I unexpectedly put away the trap, and the pigs that ate free lunch were easily caught by me."

The moral of this story is simple, when an animal depends on humans for food, its wit will be taken away, and then it will be in trouble. The same situation applies to human beings. If you want to make a person disabled, just give him a pair of crutches, and wait for a few months to achieve your goal. In other words, if you give someone a free lunch for a certain period, he/she will develop the habit of getting something for nothing. Do not forget, everyone has a need to be "taken care of" in the womb.

Yes, I always encourage you to help others, but as I always tell you, if you give a person a fish, you can only support him for one day, but if you teach him the skill of fishing, it is equivalent to supporting him for life. This old saying about fishing is very meaningful.

In my opinion, donating money is a wrong kind of help. It will make a person lose the motivation to be thrifty and diligent, and become lazy, unpredictable, and unaccountable. More importantly, when you give alms to a person, you deny his dignity, and if you deny his dignity, you take away his destiny, which is extremely immoral in my opinion. As a rich man, I have the responsibility to be a messenger for the benefit of mankind, but I cannot be the initiator of making lazy people.

Once any person develops a habit, whether it is good or bad, the habit will always possess him. The habit of eating lunch for nothing will not help a person progress, but only make him lose the chance to win. But hard work is the only reliable way out. Work is the price we pay for enjoying success. Wealth and happiness can only be obtained by hard work.

A long, long time ago, a wise old king wanted to compile a wisdom record for future generations. One day, the old king summoned his clever courtiers and said: "A mind without wisdom is like a lantern without a candle. I want you to compile a book of wisdom from all ages to illuminate the future of your children and grandchildren."

After the wise men took orders and left, they worked for a long time, finally completed a masterpiece of twelve volumes, and proudly declared: "Your Majesty, this is a record of wisdom from all ages."

The old king looked at it and said, "Sirs, I am sure that this is the crystallization of the wisdom of all ages. However, it is too thick, and people will not be able to read it. Condense it!" These smart people spent a lot of time, and after several deletions, a book was completed. However, the old king still thought it was too long and ordered them to condense again.

These smart people condensed a book into a chapter, then reduced it to a page, then turned it into a paragraph, and finally turned it into a sentence. The wise old king was very proud when he saw these words. "Gentlemen," he said: "This is really the crystallization of the wisdom of all ages, and once people everywhere know this truth, most of our problems can be solved." This saying is what we have known as: "There is no free lunch in the world."

The first and last chapter of the Book of Wisdom states that there is "no free lunch in the world". If people know that getting ahead is at the cost of hard work, most people will achieve something and at the same time will make the world a better place. And those who eat lunch for nothing will sooner or later pay the price.

To live, a person must create something within himself and the outside world that is enough to make his life and death a little dignified.

Love,
Your Father

LETTER

14

Be the foolish smart person
People who have not experienced misfortune are unfortunate.

Give a pig a good compliment, and it can climb up the tree.

A person who is smart is a fool, and a person who knows how to play a fool is smart.

(The leaders who offer high sentiments always win in the end, and get more out of their followers)

October 9, 1890

Dear John:

Tomorrow, I will go back to my hometown, Cleveland, to deal with some of our family's own affairs. I hope you can take care of some affairs for me during this period. But I remind you that if you encounter something tricky or you cannot make up your mind, you should ask Mr. Gates more for help and advice.

Mr. Gates is my most capable assistant. He is loyal and sincere, outspoken, conscientious, and shrewd. He can always help me make wise choices. I trust him very much. I believe he will be of great help to you. The premise is that you have to respect him.

Son, I know you are an outstanding graduate of Brown University, and your knowledge of economics and sociology is excellent. However, you should be clear that knowledge is originally empty, and unless knowledge is put into action, nothing will happen. Moreover, the knowledge in the textbooks is almost all compiled by writers with theoretical knowledge, hence, it is difficult to use it to help you solve practical problems.

I hope you can get rid of your dependence on knowledge and learning. This is the key to your smooth journey in life.

You need to know that learning itself is not very good. Learning must be used to make it work. To become a person who can use what you have learned, you must first become a person with practical ability.

So where does the ability to practice come from? In my opinion, it is hidden in hardship. My experience tells me that walking a difficult road – a road full of hardships, misfortunes, failures and difficulties will not only build our strong character, but also the ability to implement great things that we rely on will come into being. Those who climb out of the midst of suffering know what it means to find ways and means to save themselves. To endure hardship deliberately is one of my beliefs of success.

Maybe you might ridicule me, thinking that there is nothing more stupid than trying to experience hardship deliberately. No! People who have no experience with misfortune are unfortunate. A lot of things come and go quickly. Those who have realized their dreams of becoming famous overnight and getting rich overnight, which one of them did not disappear without a trace all of a sudden? What you get from hardship is having the ability to build your career on a solid ground, not in quicksand. People must have foresight, and only after a long period of hardship can they have a long-term harvest.

I believe you have discovered that since you came to work with me, I have not given you a heavy burden to choose. But this does not show that I doubt your ability, I just hope you are good at doing small things.

Doing small things is the cornerstone of making big things. If you are at the top from the beginning, you will not consider the mood of your subordinates, and you will not be able to use others. To survive and create achievements in this world, you must rely on manpower, that is, the power of others, but you must start from doing small things to understand the mood of being a subordinate. When you take on a higher position one day, you will know how to let them contribute all of their work enthusiasm.

Son, there are only two kinds of smart people in the world: one is smart people who use themselves, such as artists, scholars, and actors; the other is smart people who use others, such as managers and leaders. The latter needs a special ability – the ability to grasp the heart. But many leaders are clever fools. They think that in order to seize the hearts of the people, they must follow a top-down command. In my opinion, this will not only fail to gain leadership, but will reduce it by a lot. You know, everyone is very sensitive to being underestimated, and being underestimated will lose energy. Such leaders will only incapacitate subordinates.

If a pig is well praised, it can climb the tree. Managers, leaders or people who are good at driving others have always been magnanimous and they know the art of admiring others and praising others. This means they have to give emotionally. Leaders who give their deep feelings will eventually win and gain more respect from subordinates.

People without knowledge are ultimately useless, but those with knowledge are likely to become slaves of knowledge. Everyone needs to know that all knowledge will be transformed into preconceived notions, and the result will be one-sided conservative psychology, thinking that "I understand", "I understand", and "society is like this". With the prejudice of "understanding", there will be a lack of interest in knowing, and if there is no interest, it will lose the motivation to move forward, and only boredom is left waiting. Therefore, not understanding will lead to success

However, under the control of self-esteem and sense of honour, many knowledgeable people always find it difficult to "don't understand", as if asking others for advice, saying that they don't understand is a shameful thing, and even regard ignorance as a sin.

This is trying to be smart, and they will never understand this great motto – every opportunity that we don't understand will become a turning point in our lives.

A person who is smart is a fool, and a person who knows how to play a fool is really smart. If smartness is regarded as a criterion for reaping benefits, then I am obviously not a fool.

To this day, I can clearly remember a scene of pretending to be stupid. At that time, I was thinking about how to raise 15,000 dollars, and I was thinking about it when I walked on the street. Interestingly speaking, just as my mind was flashing with the idea of borrowing or borrowing money, a banker blocked my way. He whispered from the carriage: "Do you want to spend fifty thousand dollars, Mr. Rockefeller?" Am I lucky? I did not believe my ears even a slightest bit. But at that moment, I did not show even the slightest eagerness. I looked at the other person's face and told him slowly: "That's it... Can you give me twenty-four hours to think about it?" As a result, signed a loan contract with him on terms that were the most favourable to me.

Playing stupid brings you many benefits. The meaning of pretending to be stupid is to stay a low profile and become humble, in other words, to hide your cleverness. The smarter the person, the more necessary it is for them to play stupid, because as the saying goes – the more mature the rice, the more they sag.

Son, only after having hobbies can you then do it with ease. Now, start to love acting like a fool!

I expect that in the days when I am not around, it would be no easy task for you to face everything alone, but this is nothing. "Let me wait before talking" is the motto I always follow in business. I always have a habit of thinking before making a decision, I always think and judge calmly, but once I make a decision, I will implement it without hesitation. I believe you can do it too.

Love,
Your Father

LETTER

15

Wealth is the by-product of Diligence

Our wealth is a reward for our hard work.

Hard work is for oneself, not for others.

Wealth is an accident, a by-product of hard work.

(Let us go forward, firm in our faith, steadfast in our purpose; but sustained by our confidence in the will of God.)

January 25, 1907

Dear John:

I am glad to receive your letter. In your letter there were two sentences that I appreciate. One is "If you are not a winner, you are defying yourself", and the other is "Diligence brings Nobility". These two sentences are my true-life motto. If I am not self-effacing, I would like to say that they are the epitome of my life.

When talking about the huge wealth that I have created, those bad-meaning newspapers often likened me to be a very talented money-making machine. In fact, they know almost nothing about me and lack insight regarding history.

As immigrants, it is our nature to be hopeful and hardworking. When I was a child, my mother implanted the virtues of frugality, independence, diligence, trustworthiness and unremitting entrepreneurial spirit into my bones. I sincerely believe in these virtues and regard them as great success creeds. To this day, these great beliefs still flow in my blood. And all of this formed a ladder for me to climb up and sent me to the top of the mountain of wealth.

Of course, the Civil War that changed the fates and life of the American people has benefited me a lot. To be honest, it has made me a business giant that is amazing and daunting in the business world. Yes, the Civil War gave the people unprecedented business opportunities. It turned me into a rich man ahead of time. It provided me with capital support to win in the arena for grabbing opportunities that were set off after the war, and even after I was able to make money.

However, opportunities are equal as time. Why was I able I seize the opportunity to become a huge rich, while many people missed this opportunity and have to live in poverty? Is it really as my detractor said, is it because I am insatiable?

No! It is hard work! Opportunities are only reserved for hardworking people! When I was young, I believed in a law of success: wealth is an accident, a by-product of hard work. The achievement of each goal comes from diligent thinking and diligent action, and the same is true for realizing the dream of wealth.

I highly admire the phrase "Diligence brings Nobility", it is a motto that I forever will respect. Whether in the past or present, whether in North America where we are based or in the far east, those nobles who enjoy status, dignity, glory, and wealth have a never-ending heart and a pair of strong arms. Their bodies are full of perseverance and tenacious will. And it is this kind of quality or wealth that made them accomplish their careers, win respect, and become indomitable figures.

John, in this infinitely changing world, there are no permanent nobles, and no permanent poor. As you know, when I was young, I wore ragged clothes and my family was so poor that I had to rely on good-hearted people. But today I have a huge wealth empire, and I have poured huge wealth into charity. Just Like ten thousand kinds of ups and downs that rises and falls like the transformations of the world, the ups and downs are like vicissitudes of life, they multiply endlessly. People from humble and poor family backgrounds, through their hard work, persistent pursuit and wisdom, can also achieve fame and success, and become a new nobleman.

All dignity and honour must be obtained by one's own creation, so that such honour can last. But in our society today, the children of the rich are in a situation where they do not advance or retreat. Unfortunately, many of them lack the enterprising spirit, but are prone to leisure and profligacy, so even though they grew up in a wealthy environment, they die in poverty.

Therefore, you have to teach your children that if they want to perfect themselves, gain achievements, enjoy the joy of success, win the respect of society, and praise life, they can only create with their own hands; let them know that the crown of honour will only be worn on the heads of those who dare to explore; let them know that diligence is for themselves, not for others, and they are the biggest beneficiaries of diligence.

Since I was a child, I firmly believed that without hard work, there will be no fruitful and positive gains. As a child of the poor, there is no other way than to gain success, wealth and dignity through hard work. When I was in school, I was not a good student, but I was unwilling to fall behind, so I could only prepare my homework diligently and persevere. When I was ten years old, I knew I had to do as much work as I could, cutting wood, milking, fetching water, and farming. I did everything and never wasted my effort. It was the hard and toiling years in the countryside that honed my will and enabled me to withstand the hardships of starting a business in the future; it also made me more perseverant and shaped my strong self-confidence.

I know that the reason why I can always deal with adversity in the future, including my success, is largely due to the self-confidence I built since I was young.

Diligence can cultivate people's quality and abilities. When I was employed by Hewitt-Tuttle Company, I gained the reputation of being an outstanding young bookkeeper with extraordinary ability. During those days, I can be said to be wearing the stars and the moon all day long, night and day. At that time, my employer said to me that I would succeed given my extraordinary perseverance. Although I do not understand what the future will look like, there is one thing I believe, as long as I do something with my heart, I will never fail.

Today, even though I am nearly seventy years old, I still fight in the business world, because I know that the quickest way to end my life is to do nothing. Everyone has the right to choose retirement as the beginning or the end. That kind of idle attitude to life can poison people. I always think of retirement as starting again, and I have never stopped fighting for a day, because I know the true meaning of life.

John, my prominence today, the huge wealth is only the result of me putting way more strength and creativity than others. I was originally an ordinary person, and I did not have a crown on my head, but with strong perseverance, tenacity attitude, and diligence, I finally became successful. My reputation is not a false name, it is a crown cast in blood and sweat. A little bit of jealousy and shallow ignorance are all unfair to me.

Our wealth is a reward for our hard work. Let us strengthen our convictions, identify our goals, and continue our efforts with faith in God's will, my son.

Love,
Your Father

LETTER

16

Do not make excuses
Excuses are the source of failure.

The more successful a person is, the less he will make excuses.

Ninety-nine percent of failures are because people are used to making excuses.

(Ninety-nine percent of the failures come from people who have the habit of making excuse.)

April 15, 1906

Dear John:

Captain Schofield lost again. He lost and got a little furious and threw his beautiful golf club into the sky in a rage. As a result, he had to buy a new one.

Frankly speaking, I prefer the character of the captain. The goal of life is to win, and the same goes for playing basketball. So, I am going to buy a new club for him, I hope this will not be regarded as a reward for his tantrums, otherwise he will be out of control and I will be miserable.

Captain Schofield also has a commendable advantage. Although losing will make him unhappy, he believes that winning does not mean everything, and the practice of trying to win is the most important. So, after losing, he never made excuses. In fact, he can explain his loss by being too old and poor in physical strength to make himself face, but he never does that.

In my opinion, "excuses" is a mental illness, and people with this serious illness are all losers without exception. Of course, most people also have some mild symptoms. However, the more successful a person is, the less excuses he will find. The biggest difference between those who are prospering everywhere and those who do nothing is excuses.

Just pay a little attention and you will find that those who have not done anything or plan to do something, often have a basket of straw hats to explain: why he could not achieve it, why he did not do it, why he could not do it, why is he not the right person. The first action that the loser takes to settle the later events is to find various reasons for his failure.

I despise those who are good at making excuses, because it is the behaviour of the weak, but I also sympathize with them, because excuses are the cause of failure.

Once a loser finds a "good" excuse, he will hold on to it, and then always use this excuse to explain to himself and others: why he can no longer do it, why he cannot succeed. At first, he still knows how much his excuse are lies, but after repeated usage, he will become more and more convinced that it is completely true, and believe that this excuse was the real reason for his failure, and as a result his brain begins to be lazy and rigid, and the motivation to work hard to win in any way will be reduced to zero. But they never want to admit that they are a person who loves making excuses.

Occasionally, I have seen someone stand up and say: "I succeeded by my own efforts." So far, I have not seen any man or woman, dare to stand up and say: "I am the one who made myself fail." The losers have a set of excuses for themselves. They attribute their failure to family, character, age, environment, time, skin colour, religious beliefs, a certain person, and even astrology. The worst excuses are health, intelligence, and luck.

The most common excuse is health related. The sentence "my health is not good", or "I have this kind of illness" becomes a reason not to do it or to fail. In fact, no one is completely healthy, and everyone will have some physical problems.

Many people will succumb to this excuse in whole or in part, but not those who are determined to succeed. Mr. Gates once introduced me to a university professor who unfortunately lost an arm during a trip, but like every optimist I know, he still smiles a lot and helps others. When talking about his disability that day, he told me: "It's just one arm. Of course, two is better than one. But only my arm is removed, and my mind is still 100% intact and normal. I really am thankful for that."

There is an old saying that says it well: "I have been annoyed by my broken shoes until I met a man who has no feet." It is better to be grateful for your health than to complain about your discomfort. Be thankful for your health, which is able to effectively prevent various illnesses and diseases. I often remind myself: It is better to be exhausted than to let it go. Life is for us to enjoy. If we waste time worrying about our health and really fall sick, then that is the real misfortune.

The excuse of "I am not smart enough" is also very common. Almost 95% of people have this problem, just to a different degree. This kind of excuse is different, and it is usually silent. People do not publicly admit that they lack intelligence, and most of them think so deep in their hearts.

I found that most people have two basic wrong attitudes towards "intelligence": too underestimating their own brain power, and too overestimating the brain power of others. Because of these mistakes, many people despise themselves. They do not want to face challenges, because that requires considerable talent. People who think that they are stupid are really stupid. They should know that if a person does not consider the question of talent at all, and has the courage to try, he will be able to do well.

I think what is really important is not how much intelligence you have, but how to use the ingenuity you already have. To be a good businessman, you don't need to be lightning fast, you don't need to have very amazing memories, nor be amongst the best in school, the only key is to have a strong interest and enthusiasm for doing business. Interest and enthusiasm are important factors that determine success or failure.

The outcome of things is often proportional to our enthusiasm. Enthusiasm can make things a hundred times or a thousand times better. Many people do not know what enthusiasm is. The so-called enthusiasm refers to "this is amazing!" – this level of enthusiasm and drive.

I believe that an average-talented person who has an optimistic, positive and cooperative attitude towards the world will earn more money and win more respect as compared to a talented but pessimistic, passive and uncooperative person. Regardless of whether a person is dealing with trivial things, difficult tasks or important plans, as long as he is dedicated and enthusiastic to complete, the results will be far better than smart but lazy people. Because concentration and perseverance account for 95% of a person's ability.

Some people are always moaning and sighing: Why do so many talented individual fail? Here is the reason. If an extremely smart person is always using their amazing intellect to prove why things cannot succeed, instead of guiding their minds to find various ways to succeed, the fate of failure will find them. Negative thoughts have implicated their intelligence, making them unable to use their skills to accomplish anything. If they can change their mindset, I believe they will do many great things.

The brain that thinks about big things but does not know how to think is just a bucket of cheap paste.

The way of thinking that guides us to use our intelligence is far more important than the level of our intelligence. Even the highest degree of education cannot change this basic rule of success. The educational level of innate talent is not the reason behind good performance, but the management of one's thoughts. The best businessmen never have unfounded worry, but they are passionate. It is not easy to improve the quality of talent, but it is easy to improve the method of using talent.

Many people believe the so-called "knowledge is power". In my opinion, this sentence is only half right. People who use "lack of intelligence" as an excuse also misunderstood the meaning of this sentence. Knowledge is only a kind of potential power. Only when knowledge is applied constructively, then will it show its power.

There will never be a living dictionary-like character in Standard Oil because I do not need an "expert" who can only remember and cannot think. I want people who can really solve problems and come up with various ideas, who have dreams and have the courage to realize their dreams. Creative people can make money for me, but people who can only memorize information cannot.

A person who does not use talent as an excuse, never underestimates his own talents, nor does he overestimate the talents of others; He who focuses on using his assets and discovering his outstanding talents; Knows what really matters is not how much talent he has, but how he uses his existing talents and how to make good use of his talent; He will often remind himself: My mentality is more important than my intelligence; He has a strong desire to establish a "I will win" attitude; He knows to use his intellect to actively create and find ways to succeed, not to prove that he will fail; He also knows that thinking is more valuable than memorizing. He needs to use his mind to create and develop new ideas, find better new ways of doing things, and remind himself at any time: Am I using my mind to create history? Or is it just recording the history created by others?

Everything happens for a reason, and human encounters cannot happen by accident. Therefore, many people always blame bad luck for their failures. When they see others succeed, they think it is because they are too lucky. I never believe in good or bad luck, unless I think that carefully prepared plans and actions are called *luck*.

If luck decides who should do what, every business will fall apart. Assuming that Standard Oil Company wants to completely reorganize based on luck, it will put the names of all the company's employees in a big bucket, the first name drawn is the president, the second is the vice president, and so on. Isn't it ridiculous? But this is the function of luck.

I never succumb to *luck*; I believe in the law of cause and effect. Look at the people who seem to be lucky, and you will find that it is not luck, but preparation, planning and positive thinking that bring them beauty. If you look at those people with "bad luck", you will find that there are clear reasons behind them. Successful people can face setbacks, learn from failures, and create new opportunities. The mediocre people are often discouraged.

One cannot succeed by luck, but they can by paying the price of hard work. I do not want to rely on luck to win or any other good things in life, so I concentrate on developing myself and cultivating the various qualities that make myself a "winner".

Excuses keep most people out of the door to success. Ninety-nine percent of failures are because people are used to making excuses. So, in the process of pursuing career success, the most important step is to prevent yourself from making excuses.

Love,
Your Father

LETTER
17

The seeds of success is in your hands
I am my biggest capital.

My only belief is to believe in myself!

Everyone who desires to succeed should realize that the seeds of
success are sown by your side.

(Everybody has certain ideals which determine the direction of his
endeavours and his judgments.)

May 29, 1926

Dear John:

Yesterday, just yesterday, I received a letter from a young man who
aspire to become a rich man. In his letter, he urged me to answer a
question: He is lacking capital, so how can he start a business and
become rich?

My goodness, he wants me to show him the direction of his life.
But teaching others does not seem to be my specialty, and I cannot
refuse his sincerity, which is really painful. Still, I wrote back to him.
Indeed, he needed capital, but what he needed more was common
sense. Common sense is more important than money.

For a poor child who wants to start a business, they often suffer
from lack of capital. If they fear failure, they will hesitate and move

slowly like a snail, or even stop on the road to success, and never rise above others, so I specifically reminded him in my reply:

"From poverty, the road to prosperity is always unobstructed. The important thing is that you firmly believe that you are your greatest capital. You have to exercise your faith and keep exploring the reasons for your hesitation until faith replaces doubt. You have to know that you can't achieve what you don't believe in; faith is the force that drives you forward."

Everyone who desires success should realize that the seeds of success are sown by his side. As long as he recognizes this, he can get whatever he wants. In the letter, I narrated an Arab story to the young man and I believe this story will benefit others, and everyone.

The person who told me this story told me this:

There used to be a Persian, named Al Hafid, who lived not far from the Indus River. He owned a large orchid garden, hundreds of acres of fertile fields and prosperous gardens. He is a contented person and very rich – because he is rich, he is very contented with his life. One day, an old monk came to visit him and sat by his fireplace and said to him: "You are rich and you live a comfortable life, however, if you have a hand full of diamonds, you can buy the entire land in this country. And if you own a diamond mine, you can use the influence of this huge wealth to send your child straight to the throne."

After hearing the tempting words of the old monk, Hafid went to bed that night. He became a poor man – not because he lost everything, but because he became dissatisfied, so he felt poor; and because he thought he was poor, he was not satisfied. He thought: "I want a diamond mine." So, he could not sleep all night. Early the next morning he ran out to look for the monk.

The old monk was woken up early in the morning and was very unhappy. But Hafid did not care about it at all. He nonchalantly shook the old monk from his sleep and said to him: "Can you tell me where to find the diamonds?"

"Diamonds? What do you want diamonds for?"

"I want to have greater wealth," Hafid said, "but I do not know where to find diamonds."

"Oh," the old monk understood. He said, "At the mountains with a streaming river filled with white sand, there you will find the diamonds."

"Do you really think it is in such a river?"

"There are so many, more than you think there is! You just have to go out and look for it, and you will definitely find it."

"I will," Hafid said.

So, he sold the farm, recoup the funds he loaned, gave the house to his neighbours, and set out to look for diamonds.

Hafid first went to the Moonlight Mountains to look for the diamonds, then to Palestine, then to Europe, and finally he spent all his money and became worthless. Standing on the coast of Barcelona, Spain, like a beggar, he saw a huge wave surging over the pillars of Hercules. This poor, painful creature could not resist the temptation to jump and fell from the peak and ended his life.

Soon after Hafid's death, the heir to his property took the camel to the garden to drink water. When the camel stuck his nose into the clear and bottomless stream in the garden, the heir found the white sand which was gleaming in the shallow bottom of the stream. And emitting a strange light, he stretched out his hand and touched a black stone. There was a shiny spot on the stone that gave out rainbow-like colours. He took this weird stone into the house, put it on the shelf of the fireplace, and continued to work, completely forgetting about it.

A few days later, the old monk who told Hafid where to find the diamond came to visit Hafid's heir. He saw the light from the stone on the shelf, rushed over immediately, and exclaimed in surprise:

"This is the diamond! This is the diamond! Did Hafid come back?"

"No, he hasn't come back yet, and it's not a diamond either, it is just a stone, which I found in my back garden."

"Young man, you are rich! I know diamonds, these are really diamonds!"

So, they ran to the garden together and held them up with their hands. On the white sand at the bottom of the stream, many diamonds that were more beautiful and more valuable than the first one was found.

This is how people discovered the Golconda diamond mine in India. It is the largest diamond mine in human history, and its value far exceeds South Africa's Kimberly. The large Cullinan diamond inlaid on the crown of the King of England and the world's largest diamond inlaid on the crown of the Russian emperor were all mined from that diamond mine.

John, whenever I remember this story, I cannot help but sigh on behalf of Al Hafid. If Hafid stayed in his hometown and dug his own fields and gardens instead of looking in a foreign land, he would not have become a beggar, suffer from poverty and starvation, then jump into the sea and die. He already had the diamonds.

Not every story is meaningful, but this Arab story has brought me precious life lessons: your diamond is not between the distant mountains and the sea, if you are determined to dig, the diamond is in your backyard. The important thing is to sincerely believe in yourself.

Everyone has a certain ideal, which determines the direction of his efforts and judgment. In this sense, I think that a person who does not believe in himself is like a thief, because anyone who does not believe in himself and does not fully exert his abilities can be said to be a person who steals from himself; and in the process, because he is running low on creativity, he is tantamount to stealing from society. Since no one will deliberately steal from themselves, those who steal from themselves obviously did so unintentionally. However, this crime is still very serious, because the damage it causes is as great as deliberate theft.

Only by quitting this kind of stealing from ourselves can we climb to the top. I hope that the young man who is eager to make a fortune can think about the teachings contained therein.

Love,
Your Father

LETTER

18

I have no rights to be poor

I should be rich; I have no right to be poor.

Let money be my slave, but do not let me be a slave of money.

Every penny in his hand adds a penny to the power to determine his future destiny.

(Well does the man know, who has suffered, there are things sweeter and holier and more sacred than gold.)

July 26, 1906

Dear John:

There are many tragedies caused by paranoia and pride, and the same goes for people who make do with poverty.

Many years ago, at the Fifth Avenue Baptist Church, I ran into a young man named Hansen, a little gardener who lived a miserable life. Maybe Mr. Hansen thinks that it is a virtue to persist in poverty. He put on a noble appearance and said to me: "Mr. Rockefeller, I think I have a responsibility to discuss with you a question – money is the root of all evil. This is said in the Bible."

At that moment, I knew why Mr. Hansen had no relationship with wealth. He was getting life lessons from a misunderstood Bible. But he did not realize it.

I did not want this poor young man to sink deeper and deeper into his narrow-minded swamp. I told him: "Young man, I have been nurtured by various Christian maxims since I was a child and used this as my code of conduct. It is the same with you. But my memory seems to be better than you. You forgot, there is a word in front of that sentence – Love, 'loving money is the root of all evil'."

"What did you say?" Hansen's mouth was wide open, as if to swallow a whale. I really hope he has such a big appetite for money.

"Yes, young man," I patted him on the shoulder, and said, "The Bible is rooted in the dignity and love of mankind. It is a respect from the highest soul in the universe. You can quote the words without fear and entrust your life to it. Therefore, when you directly quote the wisdom of the Bible, what you quote is the truth. Loving money is the root of all evil. Loving money is only a means of worship, not the motive. If you do not have the means, you cannot achieve your goal. In other words, he who only knows to be a miser, then money is the root of all evil."

"Think about it, young man," I reminded Hansen, "If you have money, you can benefit your family and friends, give them a happy and comfortable life, and even benefitting the society, save the helpless poor people, then money will become the source of happiness."

"Young man, every penny in your hand adds a penny to the power to determine your future destiny." I persuaded him, "you should not let those paranoid ideas lock your powerful hands. You should spend time to make yourself rich because having money gets you power. And New York is full of opportunities to get rich. You should get rich, and you can get rich. Remember, young man, although you are a hurried passer-by in the world, you still have to show the light of life."

I do not know whether Hansen had accepted my advice, if not, it will be a pity, because he looks very strong and does not look like a fool.

I always thought that everyone should take time to get rich. Of course, some things are indeed more valuable than money. When we see a grave full of autumn leaves, we cannot help feeling a kind of unspeakable sadness, because I know that some things are indeed more noble than money. Especially those who have suffered deeply understand that some things are sweeter, more noble, and more sacred than gold. However, anyone with common sense knows that none of those things are not greatly improved by money. Money is not necessarily everything, but in our world, many things are inseparable from money!

Love is the greatest thing God has given us, but a lover who has a lot of money can make love happier, and money has such an ability!

If a person says, "I don't want money", it is equivalent to saying: "I don't want to serve my family, friends, and compatriots." This statement is absurd, but it is also absurd to sever the relationship between the two!

I believe in the power of money, and I believe that everyone should of course make money. However, religion has a strong prejudice against this idea because some people believe that being a poor people of God is the supreme glory. I once heard a man praying at a prayers' meeting and said that he was very grateful that he was a poor child of God. I could not help but think to myself: If this man's wife hears her husband speak such nonsense, I wonder what will happen. What do you think? She would definitely think that she married the wrong person.

I do not want to see such poor people of God again, and I do not think God wants to! I can say that if someone who should have been wealthy is weak and incompetent because of poverty, then he must have committed an extremely serious mistake; he is not only unfaithful and disloyal to himself, but also mistreating his family!

I cannot say that the amount of money earned can be used as a criterion for success in life, but almost without exception, you can use the amount of money to measure a person's contribution to society. The more your income, the more your contribution. The thought that I have enabled countless people to prosper forever, I feel that I have a great life.

I believe that God made diamonds for his people – not for Satan and alike. The only warning God has given us is that we cannot make money or earn other things in violation of God. Doing that will only add to our guilt. To get a lot of money is understandable, as long as we get it in a proper way, instead of letting money drag our noses away.

Some people have no money because they do not understand money. They think that money is cold and hard. In fact, money is neither cold nor hard – it is soft and warm, it makes us feel good, and its colour and lustre matches the clothes we wear.

The reason why I am who I am, is a creation of my past beliefs. Frankly speaking, when I felt that the world was suffering due to poverty, I had a belief: I should be a rich man and I have no rights to be poor. Over time, this belief has become as hard as steel.

When I was young, it was the time when the idea of worshiping gold was sanctified. At that time, tens of thousands of gold prospectors rushed into California with dreams of getting rich, even though it was later discovered that the gold rush was just a trap. It had greatly aroused the desire of millions of people to make a fortune, including me, a child who is only slightly older than ten years old.

At that time, my family was in a dilemma, and I often had to accept help from kind people. My mother is a very self-respecting person. She hopes that I can shoulder the responsibility of being the eldest son and build this family well. My mother's desire and teachings have cultivated a sense of responsibility that will remain unchanged throughout my life. I made my pledge: I will not become poor, I will make money, and I will use wealth to change the destiny of my family!

In the dream of getting rich in my youth, money is not just a tool for my family to lead a prosperous and worry-free life, but a society where money can be exchanged for moral dignity and social status by giving – spend wisely. These things are far more exciting to me than luxurious and magnificent residences and beautiful outfits!

My understanding of money strengthened my belief in making money and becoming a rich man, and this belief gave me incomparable fighting spirit to chase wealth.

My son, there is nothing more pitiful and contemptible than someone who makes money for the sake of making money. I know how to make money: let money be my slave, not me. This is how I did it.

Love,
Your Father

LETTER

19

Insist to be the First

Wealth is directly proportional to goal.

One is either planning to succeed or planning to fail.

For me, second place is no different from last place.

(We must march toward this goal, painfully but resolutely, certain in advance of our failings on long a road.)

March 15, 1931

Dear John:

"A person without ambition will not accomplish great things." This is what my friend, the automobile king, Mr. Henry Ford, confided to me as the secret of success when he came to see me yesterday.

I admire this rich man from Michigan very much, he is a persistent and determined guy. He has almost the same experience as mine. He has worked in farming, worked as an apprentice, and started a factory in partnership with others. Through his struggle, he eventually became one of the richest people in the United States of this era.

In my opinion, Mr. Ford is the creator of a new era. No American can completely change the American way of life like him. Just look at the cars that go back and forth on the street and you know that I am definitely not complimenting him blindly, he has turned a car from a luxury into a necessity that almost everyone can afford. And the miracle he created turned him into a billionaire. Of course, he also made my wealth grew a lot.

A person must have goals or ambitions to live, otherwise, he is like a ship without a rudder, drifting forever, and will only reach the beach of disappointment, failure, and frustration. Mr. Ford's ambition exceeds his height, and he wants to create a world where everyone can enjoy cars. This may seem unimaginable, but he succeeded. He became the owner of the global car market and made amazing profits for Ford. In the words of this guy, "It's not making cars, it's printing money." It is not difficult for me to imagine why Mr. Ford is in a good mood with his wealthy pockets and the reputation of "automobile king".

The achievements that Ford created proved one of my life credos: wealth is proportional to goals. If you have big ambitions and big goals, your mountain of wealth will rise to the sky. If you just want to pass by, then you will end up in the rat race, or even nothing, even if the wealth is close to you, you will only get a little bit of it. Before Mr. Ford succeeded, there were many automakers that were much stronger than him, but many of them went bankrupt.

People are created for a purpose. A person is either planning to succeed or planning to fail. This is the experience of my life.

I never seem to lack ambition. Since I was very young, to become the richest person has always been my impulsive ambition and dream. This seems a bit too big for a poor boy. But I think the goal must be great, because if you want to be successful, there must be stimulation. A great goal can enable you to exert all your strength, and there will be stimulation. Losing the excitement means that there is no strong force to push you forward. I often remind myself to not make any small plans, because it cannot inspire the soul.

Of course, the opportunity to become great is not like the rapid decline of the Niagara Falls, but slowly one drop at a time. The difference between greatness and close to greatness is the realization that if you expect greatness, you must work toward your goals every day.

But for a poor boy, how can this great dream become a tangible reality? Should it be achieved by working hard for others? This is a stupid idea.

I believe that working hard for myself will make me rich, but I do not believe that working hard for others will make me successful. Before I lived in Billionaires' Row (57th Street in Manhattan) I discovered that by my side, many poor people are the hardest working people. The reality is so cruel. Regardless of whether employees work hard or not, few people work for their bosses to become rich. The salary earned by working for the boss can only keep the employee alive under reasonable expectations. Although the employee may make a lot of money, it is difficult to become rich.

I have always regarded "working hard to get rich" as a lie, and never regarded working for others as a good way to accumulate considerable wealth. On the contrary, I am very convinced that working for myself can make me rich. All the actions I take are aligned to my great dream and the various goals that I continue to achieve in order to reach my goal.

When I left school and looked for a job, I set myself a goal: to go to a first-class company, to become a first-class employee. Because a first-class company will give me first-class experience, shape my first-class ability, let me grow a first-class insight, and make me a handsome income – that is the capital to create my future business, and all of this is undoubtedly the most solid cornerstone of my road to success.

Of course, working in a big company allows me to think about problems in a big company's way. This is very important. Therefore, I admire big companies, and I want to go to high-profile companies.

However, this is destined to make me suffer. I first went to a bank. I was very unlucky and was rejected; I went to a railway company again, but I still returned home in grief. The weather at that time seemed to be against me, and the heat was unbearable. But desperately, I kept searching. During that period, looking for a job became my only occupation. At 8 o'clock every morning, I tried my best to dress myself up, and then I left my residence to start a new round of appointment interviews. For several weeks, I ran the companies on the list, but I still found nothing.

This looks terrible, doesn't it? But no one can stop you from moving forward. The person who hinders you the most is yourself. You are the only one who can go on forever. I warned myself: if you do not want others to steal your dreams, then you stand up immediately after being knocked down by setbacks. I was not frustrated or discouraged, but continuous setbacks strengthened my determination. I started from scratch again, running one by one, and a few companies even let me run two or three times.

God never abandoned me. This indomitable job-hunting journey finally ended in one afternoon six weeks later. On September 26, 1855, I was hired by the Hewitt-Tuttle Company.

This day seemed to determine everything in my future. To this day, whenever I ask myself what would happen if I did not get the job, I often tremble all over. Because I know what I got from that job, and what will happen to me without it. Therefore, I have celebrated September 26th as a "rebirth birthday" all my life, and I have more emotions for this day than my birthday.

At this point, I am moved by myself.

Humans function like a bicycle, unless you move up and forward towards the target, you will stagger and fall. Three years later, I left the Hewitt-Tuttle company with abilities and self-confidence beyond ordinary people, and co-founded Clark – Rockefeller with Mr. Clark, and started the history of working for myself.

Stupidly hard work may still get nothing after all the hard work, but if you think of working hard for your boss as a ladder to serve yourself one day, it is undoubtedly the beginning of wealth creation. The feeling of being your own boss is so great, it is beyond words.

Of course, I cannot always be immersed in the pride of being amongst the trade agents at the age of 18. I warned myself: "Your future depends on the days that pass by. Your end goal in life is to be the richest man in the United States. Where are you? It is still far, far away. You must continue to work hard for yourself." Being the richest person is the basis for my efforts and the strength to spur myself. In the past few decades, I have always been a believer in the pursuit of excellence. The one sentence I most often motivates myself with is: For me, second place is no different from last place. If you understand it, you will think that it is not surprising that I ruled the oil industry as the indisputable king.

Each of us lives in hope, but I live more in the achievement of my goals. My goal in life is to be the number one. This is also the life plan that I try to make and abide by. All my efforts and actions are loyal to my life goals and life rules.

God gave us smart minds and strong muscles, not to make us losers, but to make us great winners. Twenty years ago today, the Federal Court disbanded our happy family, but whenever I think of the achievements I have created, I get excited.

A great life is the process of conquering excellence. We must move forward to this goal, not be afraid of pain, be resolute, and be prepared to fall on the long road.

Love,
Your Father

LETTER

20

Take risks to make use of opportunities

The higher the risk, the greater the return.

The more things you have, the greater your power.

To win, you must understand the value of risk, and you must have your own vision of creating luck.

(Our lives begin to end the day we become silent about things that matter.)

November 2, 1936

Dear John:

Tomorrow, or perhaps before tomorrow, there will be a person who will live a rich life. It was reported in the newspaper that his name is David Morris, who has the same last name as Mr. Robert Morris. David Morris was the financial director during the American Revolution and the Prince of Commerce in Philadelphia, and recently had a streak of good luck at the casino and won a lot of money. He also said that he was a master at the casino. At the same time, he posted a life motto of a gambler: Only by curiosity can you discover opportunities, and by taking risks can you make use of them.

You know, I always disagree with people who are addicted to gambling, but I cannot help but admire this gentleman. I even believe that with his philosophical wisdom and mind, he might become a very successful businessmen – an excellent gambler, if he joins the business world.

I make such an appreciative assumption, not to say that good gamblers will become good businessmen. In fact, I hate those who treat the industry as casinos, but I do not disagree with the adventurous spirit because I know a rule: "The higher the risk, the greater the return." For everyone, sailing in the business sea is the greatest adventure that life can provide him.

The trajectory of my life is a rich adventure. If I were to find out which adventure was most decisive and the most relevant to my future, it would be entering the oil industry.

Before investing in the oil industry, our own bank, agricultural product agency sales, was doing a good job, and I was fully expected to become a big middleman if we were to continue. But all this were changed by Mr. Andrews, an expert in lighting. He told me: "John, when kerosene burns, the light is brighter than any lighting oil. It will definitely replace other lighting oils. Think about it. Well, John, how big of a market will that be. If we can step foot into it, what will it be like!"

The more things I have, the greater the power. The opportunity is here, letting it go is not just about money, but it also weakens your power in the arena of getting rich. I told Andrews: "I do!" We invested 4,000 dollars, which was a lot of money for us, and started an oil refining business. When the money is invested, I did not think about failure, although at that time, while oil made many millionaires, it also turned more people into paupers.

I plunged into the oil refining industry and worked hard. In less than a year, oil refining earned us more profits than agricultural products and became the company's largest business. At that moment, I realized that it was courage and adventurous spirit, that opened up a new way of making money.

At that time, no industry was able to get rich overnight like the oil industry. Such a prospect greatly stimulated my desire to make big money, and it also allowed me to see the long-awaited opportunity to make big plans. I warned myself: "You must hold on to it tightly, it can bring you to the realm of your dreams."

But then I aggressively expanded the business strategy of the oil industry and irritated my partner Mr. Clark. Clark is an ignorant, conceited, weak, and lacking courageous person. He is afraid of failure and advocates a prudent business strategy, which is completely contrary to my business ideology. In my eyes, money is like dung. If you scatter it around, you can do a lot of things, but if you hide it, it will be just an unbearable foul-smelling asset. Clark is not a good businessman; he does not know the true value of money.

When we are indifferent to important things, our lives will come to an end. Clark has become a stumbling block on my road to success, and I must kick him away-and break up with him. This is an important moment.

To win, you must understand the value of risk, and you must have your own vision of creating luck. For me, breaking up with Mr. Clark is undoubtedly a risky adventure. Before I decide to throw everything into the oil industry, I must be sure that oil will not disappear. At that time, many people believed that oil was a blooming epiphany, which was difficult to last. I certainly hope that the oil source will not be exhausted, as once there is no oil source, those investments will be worthless, and my fate may be worse than that of gamblers in the casino. But the information I received made me optimistic that the oil source will not disappear. Hence, it is time to break up.

Before the announcement to Mr. Clark, I first pulled Mr. Andrews over in private. I said to him: "We are going to be lucky. There is a sum of money waiting for us, and that is a large sum of money. I want to terminate my relationship with the Clark Brothers. If I buy their shares, will you be in it with me?" Andrews did not let me down. A few days later, I got even more support from the banks.

In February that year, after a series of preparations, I proposed to break off with Mr. Clark. Although he was reluctant, I have decided.

Finally, we all agreed to auction the company to the buyer with the highest price.

To this day, when I think of the auction scene, I feel very excited. It feels like gambling in a casino, which is thrilling and made me completely focused on it. It was a good bet. What I bet with is money, but what I gamble with is my life.

The company started the auction from 500 dollars, but it quickly climbed to several thousand dollars, and then slowly climbed to 50,000 dollars. This price has exceeded my estimate of the value of the refinery. But the bidding price continued to rise, as it started to exceed 60,000 dollars, and then soared to 70,000 dollars. At this time, I began to fear. I was worried about whether the company created by me, could still be bought back and whether it was valued that high. But I calmed down quickly, and I warned myself at a lightning speed: "Don't be afraid, since you have made up your mind, you have to go forward!" The competitor offered 72,000 dollars, and I did not hesitate to offer 72,500 dollars. At this time, Mr. Clark stood up and shouted: "I won't add it anymore, John, it belongs to you!"

Dear John, that was the moment that decided my life, and I felt its extraordinary significance.

Of course, I paid a high price for buying out Mr. Clark. I gave Clark half of the agency's shares and seventy-two thousand five hundred dollars. But what I won was freedom and a glorious future. I became my own master, my own employer, and I no longer had to worry about those short-sighted mediocre people blocking my way.

When I was 21 years old, I owned the largest refinery in Cleveland, and became one of the largest refiners in the world. Today, thinking about it, this guy who consumes 500 barrels of crude oil a day was undoubtedly the weapon that brought me to the path of hegemony and allowed me to conquer the oil kingdom. Thanks to that auction, it was the beginning of my success in life.

It is almost certain that safety first cannot make us rich. If we want to get paid, we must always accept the necessary risks that follow. Isn't life like this?

There is no such thing as maintaining the status quo. If you do not advance, you will retreat. It is that simple. In my aspect, being cautious is not the perfect way to succeed. No matter what we do, or even our lives, we must choose between taking risks and being cautious. And sometimes, the chance of winning by taking risks is much greater than by being cautious.

Merchants are chasers of profits and wealth. They rely on creating resources and obtaining resources from others, and even forcing others to give up resources to make themselves rich. Therefore, taking risks is an indispensable means for merchants to conquer the market.

If you want to know the tricks that are risky but does not incur failure, you only need to remember one sentence: plan boldly and implement carefully.

Love,
Your Father

LETTER
21

Insult is a kind of motivator

Insult is a measure of ability.

Never let your own personal prejudices hinder your success.

You believing and being in harmony with yourself, will make yourself the most faithful companion.

(It is the task of men of thought, as well as men of action to know to how to put aside pride and prejudice.)

February 27, 1901

Dear John:

Your performance when negotiating with Mr. Morgan surprised me and your mother. We did not expect you to have the courage to confront the Wall Street's domineer. Moreover, you dealt with him with calamity, eloquence, well-mannered, and still have complete control over your opponent. Thank God for allowing us to have such an outstanding child like you.

You told me in a letter that Mr. Morgan treated you rudely, and intentionally wanted to insult you. I think you are right. In fact, you wanted to retaliate on the behalf of me and be humiliated instead.

You know, Morgan proposed to form an alliance with me this time because he was worried that I would pose a threat to him. I believe he is reluctant to cooperate with me, because he knows that we are carriages running on a two-way street, and neither of them likes each other. I feel sick whenever I see his arrogance. I think there are also areas where he will feel uncomfortable when he sees me too.

But Morgan is a business wizard. He knows that I pay no attention to Wall Street, and he is not afraid of his threat to me. Therefore, if he wants to realize his ambition to rule the US steel industry, he must cooperate with me. Otherwise, waiting for him would be a competition involving life and death.

People who are good at thinking and good at action know that arrogance and prejudice must be eliminated, and they all know that they can never let their own personal prejudices hinder their success. Mr. Morgan is such a person. So even though Mr. Morgan did not want to deal with me, he still asked me if he could meet him in the office of the President of Standard Oil Company.

Those who can hold on to the last minute in the negotiation will definitely reap the benefits, so I told Morgan: "I have retired. If you want, I will be happy to wait for you in my home." He really came, and it was him in person. This is obviously a bit condescending to him. But he never dreamed that when he asked specific questions, I would say: "I am very sorry, Mr. Morgan, I am retired. I think my son, John, will be happy to talk to you about that deal."

Only a fool cannot tell I was blatantly scorning Morgan, but he was very respectful and told me that he hoped you could talk to him in his Wall Street office. I agreed.

Revenge on others is an attack on yourself. Mr. Morgan did not seem to understand this truth, but in order to relieve his anger, he instead let you control it instead. But in any case, even though Mr. Morgan blatantly insulted me, he always kept his eyes on the goal to be achieved, which I do admire.

My son, we grew up in a society that pursued dignity, and I know what it means to be insulted to a person who loves dignity. But in many cases, no matter who you are, even the President of the United States of America is unable to prevent insults coming from others.

So, what should we do? Do we fight back in rage and defend your dignity? Or is it to be tolerant and generous? Or do you respond in other ways?

As you may remember, I have always cherished a group photo of my middle school classmates. I am not in the photo, only children from wealthy families. Decades have passed, but I still treasure it, and especially the scene in the photo.

It was one afternoon, and the weather was good. The teacher told us that a photographer came to take pictures of the students in class. I have taken pictures, but very few. For a child from a poor family, taking pictures is a luxury. As soon as the photographer appeared, I imagined how I wanted to be photographed, to smile more, be more natural, act handsomely, and even started to imagine as if I was going home to report a piece of good news to my mother: "Mom, I took a picture! Yes! The photographer took my photo, great!"

I stared at the photographer who was bent with excitement in my eyes, hoping that he would pull me into the view of the camera soon. But I was disappointed. The photographer seemed to be an aestheticist. He straightened up, pointed at me, and said to my teacher: "Can you ask that student to leave his seat? His clothes are really too shabby." I was a weak student and had to obey the teacher's orders. I can't fight, I can only stand up silently and let the well-dresses students create a beautiful scenery.

At that moment I felt my face hot. But I was not angry, and neither did I pity myself, nor did I lament at my parents for not dressing me more properly. In fact, they did their best for me to get a good education. Looking at the adjusting the camera scene, I clenched my fists in my heart and swore to myself: One day, you will become the richest person in the world! What is the point of having a photographer take a picture of you! Having the world's most famous painter paint you a portrait would then be considered a pride of its own!

My son, my vow at that time has become a reality! In my eyes, the meaning of the word insult has changed. It is no longer a sharp blade that strips me off dignity, but a powerful driving force, like overwhelming mountains, urging me to move ahead and pursue all good things. If the photographer inspired a poor boy to become the richest man in the world, it does not seem like he went overboard.

Everyone enjoys applause and praises. It is either affirming our achievements, or affirming our quality, ethics and morality; when we are attacked, insulted or suffered from another's malice, I think the reason we are being insulted is because of our poor ability. This ability may be related to our character or the way we are doing things. In short, it does not constitute respect for others. So, I want to say that humiliation is not a bad thing. If you are a person who knows how to reflect calmly, you might think that humiliation is a measure of ability. That is what I did.

I know that any slight insult can hurt dignity. However, dignity is not given by God, nor is it given by others. It is your own creation. Dignity is a spiritual product that you enjoy yourself. Everyone's dignity belongs to him. If you think you have dignity, you have dignity. So, if someone hurts your feelings and your dignity, you have to stay calm. If you do not cling to your dignity, no one can hurt you.

My son, your relationship with yourself is the beginning of all relationships. When you believe in yourself and are in harmony with yourself, you are your most faithful partner. Only in this way, will you stay indifferent.

Love,
Your Father

LETTER

22

Using your strength to scare your opponents

The more you think you can do it, the smarter you will get.

When it comes to money, never mention the amount first.

When you are in business, you must not want all the money for yourself, but keep a little money for others to earn.

(I believe that the world can be changed by man's endeavour, and that this endeavour can lead to something new and better.)

February 27, 1901

Dear John:

I met with the mediator Henry Frick tonight, and I told him: "Just as my son told Mr. Morgan, I am not in a hurry to sell the United Mining Company. But as you guessed, I will never prevent the establishment of any business that has value. However, I firmly oppose the actions of condescension buyers and set prices in attempts to prevent them from excluding us. I would rather fight to the end than to do such a business." I asked Mr. Frick to tell Mr. Morgan, he is in the wrong.

John, it seems that you have to continue dealing with Mr. Morgan, even though you hate him. So, I want to give you some suggestions to let the invincible guy know what the evil result of doing things his own.

Son, many people make the same mistake. They do not know what they are doing. In fact, no matter which industry you are engaged in, such as oil refinery, real estate, steel business, or being a president or employee, you are all engaged in one industry, that is, dealing with people. Negotiation is even more so, it is not the business that is at war with you, but the people!

Therefore, a true understanding of yourself and your opponents are the prerequisites for ensuring that you win a big victory in a match. You need to know that preparation is part of the psychology of the game, and you must know yourself and the enemy. If you want to have a substantial advantage, you must know:

First, the overall environment: what is the market situation and what is the business situation.

Second, your resources: what are your strengths and weaknesses, and what capital do you have.

Third, the opponent's resources: what are the opponent's assets, and where are his strengths and weaknesses. In any competition, one of the important factors in planning a grand strategy is to understand the strengths of the opponent.

Fourth, your goal and attitude: The motto of the god of sun, Apollo, is only a short sentence: "You know yourself." You need to know what you are doing, what goals you have, and how determined you are to achieve them. Like a winner, I still doubt my own strengths and weaknesses in spirit and attitude.

John, you have to remember my saying: The more you think you can do it, the brighter you will become, and a positive attitude will create success.

Fifth, the opponent's goals and attitudes: try to judge the opponent's goals, and it is also important to try to penetrate the opponent's heart and understand his thoughts and feelings.

There is no doubt that the last one – predicting and understanding your opponent – is the most difficult to put to use, but you have to strive to achieve it. Most of those great military generals have a habit. They always try their best to understand the opponent's character and habits in order to judge the opponent's possible moves and direction of action. In all competitive activities, it is always useful to be able to understand the opponent and the competitor, because then you can predict the opponent's movements. Proactively and anticipatory measures are almost always more effective and more powerful than passive reactions. As the saying goes, prevention is better than cure.

In some cases, your competitors may be people you know well, then you have to take advantage of this. If you understand that he is a very cautious person, perhaps you better be careful yourself; if you feel that he is always impulsive, perhaps this is suggesting you to be bold, otherwise you may be driven to a corner by them.

However, you do not have to be familiar with your opponents to understand them. As long as you can see the details, you can find many valuable things at the negotiating table. People who are good at negotiating should be able to observe everything. You do not even have to wait until for your first step to get to know your opponent.

What we say may reveal or conceal our own thoughts, but our choices almost always reveal our inner secrets-thoughts, the first choice everyone makes is also the first revelation. In a negotiation, you must understand what you are saying. If you can really control everything, you should be able to control what you are saying and bring yourself benefits.

Similarly, you must remain vigilant at all times in order to receive messages from your opponents. If so, you can continue to control a clear advantage. If you fail to do this, you may lose another opportunity. You need to know that losing in a competitive negotiation means that your chances of winning the negotiation next time will be reduced.

The secret of trading is that you need to know what can and cannot be traded. Mr. Morgan sees us as debris in the corner to be swept out, but we must stay on the floor. This cannot be debated. At the same time, he must also give a good price. But you also need to know that when doing business, you must not think of making a clean profit, but to leave some for others to earn.

John, you know, we are willing to make this transaction because we think it is good for us. This is obvious. However, you should not be subjected to such a clear and narrow perspective.

Too many "smart people" think that the purpose of the brand is not to trade, but to pick up a bargain, hoping to buy things at the lowest price. This time, the price offered by Morgan is more than a million lower than the actual valuation. If he only wants to make this kind of transaction, it means that he will lose his chance to ascend the ladders of the US steel industry. The essence of the transaction is exchange value, exchange what others want for what you want.

The best way to achieve a good deal is to emphasize its value. And many people make the mistake of emphasizing price instead of value. What they often say: "This is really cheap, and you can never find such a low price." Yes, no one wants to pay a high price, but beyond the lowest price, people want the highest value.

John, in your negotiations with Mr. Morgan, when it comes to money, you must never mention the amount first, but provide him with-precious value and emphasize what he can buy from you.

I believe that people can change the world through hard work and reach a new and better state. I wish you all the best!

Love,
Your Father

LETTER

23

There must be a spirit of cooperation
Treat others the way you wish to be treated.

A friendship built on business is far better than a business built on friendship.

Be nice to others when you climb up, because you will run into them when you go downhill.

(The essence of life is struggle and competition. Struggle and competition are stimulating.)

May 16, 1901

Dear John:

You and Mr. Morgan finally shook hands. This is the greatest handshake in American economic history. I believe the future generations will remember this great moment generously, because, as the Wall Street Journal said, it holds the meaning of "a super battleship built by Wall Street tycoons and oil tycoons has set sail. It will be unstoppable and will never sink."

John, do you know what this is called? This is the power of cooperation.

Cooperation, in the eyes of those with arrogance, it may be a weak or shameful thing, but in my opinion, cooperation is always a smart choice provided that it is beneficial to me. Now, I would like you to know of a fact:

If it is not God who gave me what I have accomplished today, I would like to attribute it to the support from three powers: The first power comes from following the rules, which allows the enterprise to operate continuously; the second force comes from cruel and ruthless competition, it makes every competition more perfect; the third force comes from cooperation, which allows me to obtain benefits and profit from cooperation.

And the reason why I can run ahead of the competition is that I am good at taking shortcuts—cooperating with others. At every stop of my journey to create wealth, you can see the signs of cooperation. Because from the day I set foot in society, I knew that at anytime, anywhere, as long as there is competition, no one can fight alone, unless he wants to kill himself, a smart person will form a cooperative relationship with others, including competitors, under the guise of others to survive or become stronger.

Of course, I can make a hypothesis that is likely to come true. If we do not collaborate with Mr. Morgan, both parties are likely to fight to the end with both sides losing, while our opponent, Mr. Carnegie, will profit from and continue the trend of dominating the steel industry. But now, Mr. Carnegie must be beating himself up. Think about it, who can be calm when his opponent cannibalizes his territory? Unless he is a dead man lying in the grave.

Cooperation can suppress or eliminate the opponent and achieve the goal of making oneself stride towards their goal. In other words, cooperation is not necessarily the pursuit of victory. Unfortunately, only a few people understand the marvel within it.

However, cooperation is not the same as friendship, love, and marriage. The purpose of cooperation is not to gain emotions, but to gain benefits and an advantage. We should know that success depends on the support and cooperation of others. There is a gap between our ideals and ourselves, and we must bridge this gap. In order to fill this gap, we must rely on the support and cooperation of others.

Of course, I will never refuse to establish friendship with business partners. I believe that friendship built on business is far better than business built on friendship. For example, my collaboration with Mr. Henry Flagler. Henry is my eternal confidant and best assistant; By forming an alliance with him, he not only provided me with investment, but also wisdom and spiritual support. Like me, Henry was never complacent and ambitious. It was his dream to become the master of the oil industry. Until now, I still remember the scene when we first started cooperating. At that time, except for eating and sleeping, we were almost inseparable. We would pretty much do everything together, thinking together, going and leaving work together, making plans together, motivating each other, and sharing the same determination. During that time, just like spending a honeymoon, it will always be a happy memory for me.

Now, decades later, we are still as close as brothers, and I will not sell this emotion for much money. Therefore, I insist that you call him Uncle Henry instead of Mr. Henry.

I never try to buy and sell friendship because friendship cannot be bought with money. Behind every friendship requires genuine support. The reason why Henry and I have an unregrettable cooperation and eternal friendship is not only because we are conspirators in pursuit of interests, but more importantly, we are all self-disciplined people, and we all know the value of "treating others the way you want to be treated, starts from now".

"Do not do unto others as you would that they should do unto you." is not only my code of conduct, but also my wise attitude towards cooperation. Therefore, I never bully weak opponents with money. I prefer to talk to them, and I am unwilling to take a domineering posture to suppress them. Otherwise, I may ruin our cooperation and stop the goal in the middle.

Of course, when I meet an arrogant and rude person, I cannot forget to humiliate him. For example, I once taught Mr. Vanderbilt, the owner of the New York Central Railroad a lesson.

Vanderbilt was born a nobleman, made military exploits in the Civil War, and enjoyed the title of General. However, he regarded the honours he received on the battlefield as an indispensable capital in his life, and he thought that he held the power of transportation, so he could treat us as part-timers.

Once, Henry went up him to talk about transportation, but who knew that this arrogant guy said: "Young man, you want to talk to me? Your rank seems lower!" Henry has never been insulted like this, but at that moment, his good upbringing helped him. He did not lose his mind, but when he returned to the office, his beautiful pen holder suffered, and fell to pieces.

I quickly comforted him: "Henry, forget what the dog piss said, I will definitely return you your dignity." Later, Vanderbilt was anxious to do business with us and asked us to negotiate with him. I sent someone to tell him: "Yes, but you have to come to our office to talk." As a result, this general who was accustomed to others' flattering and pleasing him could only condescend to meet a young man who was more than forty years younger than him, and at the same time succumb to the conditions put forward by the two young men. I think, at that moment, General Vanderbilt must have understood this truth: Be nice to others when you climb up, because you will meet them when you go downhill.

I hate treating people with a rude attitude, and I know that being patient and gentle to subordinates and colleagues are helpful in achieving goals. I know that you can buy talents with money, but it will not buy people's hearts, but when you show respect when you pay, they will serve you faithfully. This is where I can build an efficient management team.

But I do not want to make wrong judgments because of this, thinking that cooperation will make me a good person. No.

Cooperation is not a question of being a good person, but a question of benefits and interests. No alliance is permanent, and cooperation is just a profitable tactic. When the environment changes, the tactics will change accordingly, otherwise, you will lose. The reality is harsh, you have to be tougher, but obviously you also have to be a good person.

John, the essence of life is struggle and competition. They are exciting. However, when they develop into conflicts, they are often devastating and destructive, and timely cooperation can resolve them.

Love,
Your Father

LETTER

24

Not to be outdone will win

The size of our thoughts determines the size of our achievements.

Attitude is our best friend and also our worst enemy.

The road to success is paved with gold, but this road is only a one-way street.

(Optimism is a belief that life will be, in the long run, more good than bad, that even when bad things happen, the good will eventually outbalance them.)

July 19, 1897

Dear John:

It is wonderful to be immersed in warm and sincere love. Today, students from the University of Chicago allowed me to experience this wonderful feeling. For the time being, I consider it as a reward for my creation of this institution, but it did make me overjoyed.

Sincerely speaking, before I decided to invest in the establishment of this university, I never expected to be treated like a saint. My original intention was just to do something to pass on our best culture to the younger generation, to create a better future for our youth, and our younger generation. It now appears that my goal has been achieved. This is the wisest investment I have made in my life.

The young people at the University of Chicago are very cute. They have a beautiful vision for the future, and they all have the motivation to achieve something. A few of them with childish faces came up to me and said that I am their role model, and sincerely hoped that I can give them some advice. I accepted their request, and advised the future Rockefellers:

Success is not measured by a person's height, weight, education, or family background, but by the *size* of his thoughts. The *size* of our thoughts determines the *size* of our achievements. The most important of all is that we must value ourselves, overcome the greatest weakness of mankind – self-deprecation, and never sell ourselves cheaply. You are greater than you think, so you should expand your thinking to the extent to your fullest potential, and never underestimate yourself.

At this time, applauses suddenly sounded. I was obviously completely captured by it. I was so overwhelmed that I could not control my tongue. I continued:

For thousands of years, many philosophers have advised us: Know yourself. However, most people interpret it as just knowing the negative side of themselves. Most self-assessments include too many shortcomings, mistakes, and incompetence. It is good to recognize your own shortcomings and you can use this to seek improvement. However, if we only recognize the negative side of ourselves, we will fall into chaos and make ourselves worthless.

For those who long for others to respect them, the reality is cruel, because others will think of him the same way he thinks of himself. We will all be treated like "what we think we are". Those who think that they are a bit worse than others, no matter what their actual ability is, will definitely be a bit worse than others, because the mind itself can regulate and control various actions.

If a person feels that he is inferior to others, he will show "true" actions that are inferior to others; and this feeling cannot be hidden or concealed. Those who think they are "not very important" will eventually become "not very important" people.

On the other hand, those who believe that they have the "capability of taking heavy responsibilities" will really become a "very important" person. Therefore, if you want to be an important person, you must first make yourself believe that "I am really important", and you have to truly feel that way before others will follow.

No one can escape the principle of reasoning: how you think will determine how you act, and how you act will determine how others think about you. Just like your own success plan, it is actually very simple to gain the respect of others. In order to be respected by others, you must first feel that you are indeed worthy of respect, and the more you respect yourself, the more others will respect you.

Please think about it: Do you respect those who wander in the dilapidated streets? Of course not. Why? Because those rascals do not value themselves at all, they will only let their inferiority corrode their souls and eventually give up on themselves.

A person's self-esteem is the core of his personality. What kind of person you think you are, will make you become that person.

Everyone, no matter where he lives, whether he is unknown or prominent, civilized or barbaric, young or old, has a strong desire to become an important person. Please think carefully about everyone around you – your neighbours, yourself, your teachers, your classmates, your friends, who does not have a strong desire to hold a lot of power? All of them do, and the desire is the strongest and most urgent goal that is being pursued by mankind.

However, why do people often turn this achievable goal into an unachievable dream? In my opinion, it is due to attitude. Attitude is the materialization of each of our thoughts and spiritual factors, and it determines our choices and actions. In this sense, attitude is our best friend and also our worst enemy.

I admit that we cannot control the direction of the wind, but we can adjust the sail – in other words, choosing our attitude. Once you choose to value your own attitude, those cowardly thoughts that degrade yourself, demoralize your will, corrodes your confidence and encourages you to give up on yourself such as "I am a useless person, I am a nobody, I have no say, I am worthless", and so on, will disappear and be replaced by the resurrection of the mind, proactive changes in thoughts and actions, increase of confidence, and usage of the "I can! And I will!" mentality to face everything.

Boys! If any of you ever lied to yourself, please stop here, because those who do not think that they are important are ordinary people who give up on themselves. Do not demean yourself at any time, you must first choose your own assets – or advantages. Ask yourself: "What are my strengths?" When analysing your strengths, you cannot be too kind.

You have to focus on your strengths and tell yourself that you are better than you think. You must have a foresight and see the future potential for development, instead of just looking at the current situation, and having lofty expectations of yourself. Always remember this question: "Will important people do this?" This will gradually make you more successful.

Children, the road to success is paved with gold, but this road is just a one-way street. At this moment, we need an optimistic attitude. Optimism is often called *hope* by philosophers. Let me first tell you that this is a misunderstanding of optimism! The so-called optimism is a kind of belief, that is, believing that life is ultimately more joyful and less miserable, and that even if things that are not as good as we wish, good things will eventually prevail.

John, do you know? In my impromptu speech in just ten minutes, I actually received eight rounds of applauses. It is a pity that too much applause interfered with my chain of thoughts. I have an important point that was driven away by the applause, that is, improving your thinking ability will help you improve the standards of various actions and makes them more effective. But I am still very happy, that my tongue actually carries such a big charm.

Love,
Your Father

LETTER

25

Have every penny brings you benefits
Make every penny's worth.

Do not take the first step without thinking about the last step.

Creativity, spontaneity, and belief can turn the impossible into a possibility.

(I have never looked upon ease and happiness as ends in themselves, I call it the ideal of a pigsty.)

June 21, 1914

Dear John:

Mr. Charles left us forever, which makes me sad. As a faithful citizen of God, Mr. Charles has always been a very kind and rich man. He is willing to do good, and constantly uses the money he earns to help those compatriots suffering in poverty. I believe that God will welcome him with a smile in heaven because of his benevolence and selflessness.

Being with a sincere soul is a blessing from heaven. It is a lifetime honour to have a partner like Mr. Charles. Of course, Mr. Charles's cautious character often leads to constant friction between us but it does not take away my respect for him at the very least. To lose respect for noble people is to deprive yourself of dignity.

Back then, the top management of the company had the habit of having lunch together. Every time I had a meal, even though I was the first person in the company, I would leave him a seat that symbolized the core of the company to show my respect for his integrity. Yes, this is not enough, noble morality should be praised. On the whole, although this is only a very small detail, it may affect the entire company and affect the company's performance.

In fact, Standard Oil's partners are all honest people. We all know how valuable and important cooperation is to respect, trust, and unite. We strive to make it a reality. Therefore, even if there is a disagreement, we will only speak up and talk about the matter, not scheme against one another, or make false claims. I believe that in such a pure atmosphere, even if someone has improper thoughts, he will leave them at home.

But this is just one of the reasons why Standard Oil is so powerful that it awes its opponents, while sincere corporation is regarded as the most important factor in our lives. In this regard, Mr. Charles exemplified his practice.

As the leader of the company, I sincerely advocated this during a board meeting: "We are a family, we share the honour and disgrace, and our strong palms hold up our common cause. Therefore, I suggest to everyone, please do not say what I should do, but say what we should do. Don't forget, we are partners, and whatever we do is for the benefit of all of us."

My speech infected Mr. Charles, and he was the first to respond to me: "Gentlemen, I understand, what John meant was that "we" are more important than "me", we are a family! That is right! It should be "we"!

At that moment, I saw our great future because we began to be loyal to "us". Do not forget that everyone is selfish, everyone is loyal to themselves by nature, and "I" is the religion in everyone's heart. When "we" replaces "me", the power it gives off will be incalculable. The reason why I can achieve great success is because I manage everyone first, every single one of them.

Mr. Charles and I share a common belief, and we are both devout Christians. I like Mr. Charles's favourite motto: "Treasure time and money." I always thought it was a motto that embodies great wisdom. I believe that most people will like it, but it is difficult to turn it into their own thoughts, beliefs, and values, and permanently integrate it into their own blood.

Yes, no matter how much a person accumulates wise words and proverbs, and no matter how high his insights are, if he cannot use every right opportunity to act, his character will not be well influenced in the end. If you lose your good intentions, you will get nothing.

Almost everyone knows that whether you can build a happy life and achieve success is related to how you use your time. However, for many people, time is their enemy. They kill it and obliterate it; but if anyone steals their time, they will be furious, because time is money after all, and the most important time is life. Unfortunately, they just do not know how to use their time.

In fact, this is not as difficult as Mr. Columbus discovering America. The important thing is that we plan every day, even every moment, know what to think about and how to act. Planning is the basis for us to live in accordance with the daily situation, and it can show us what is feasible. To make a perfect plan, you must first confirm what you want; in addition, every plan must have measures and you have to monitor the results. A plan that can discuss actions and produce results is a valuable plan. Of course, creativity, spontaneity and belief can turn the impossible into possible and break through the limits of a plan, so do not be strictly confined within the plan.

Every moment is the key, and every decision affects the course of life, so we must have a determined strategy. Resolution should not be made too hastily when encountering important problems, if you do not think about the last step, never take the first step. Believe that there is always time to think about the problem and act, and you need to have patience to allow maturity of the plan. But once a decision is made, it must be implemented faithfully like a fighter.

Making money will not make you bankrupt; it is Mr. Charles's bible for getting rich. At a luncheon, Mr. Charles publicized his philosophy of making money. That day, he inspired each of us with passion like a motivational speaker would. He told us all: There are two kinds of people in the world that will never be rich:

First, people who like to live a glamorous life, like flies staring at a stinky meat. They are very interested in luxury goods. They spend so much that they do their best to have exquisite costumes, expensive cars, luxurious houses, and highly sought-after art. This kind of life is indeed fascinating, but it lacks rationality, and they lack such vigilance: They are looking for ways to increase debt, and they will become poor slaves to cars and houses, and once they go bankrupt, they are finished!

The second type of people, are those who like to save money, and store it in the bank, but it is no different from freezing money. You must know that you cannot make money on interest.

However, there is a kind of people who will become rich. For example, everyone here. We do not look for ways to spend money but look for ways to cultivate and manage various investments, because we know that wealth can be used to produce more money. We will use the money to invest and create more wealth. But we also need to know that every penny can bring benefits! This is just like John's usual business principle – make every penny's worth!

Mr. Charles' speech drew enthusiastic applause. I was ignited by him, and I was applauding so hard, that I still felt two palms aching after the meal.

Now, I can no longer hear that kind of applause, and there is no chance for that kind of applause. But "treasure time and money" has always accompanied me. I have no reason to waste my life. Wasting my life is tantamount to ruining myself. There is no greater tragedy in

the world than ruining myself. I do not regard ease and pleasure as
the purpose of life, because I call them the ideal of a pigsty.

Love,
Your Father

LETTER
26

Patience is the strategy
Impulse is always our worst enemy.

Only when you can endure what people cannot, can you then do what people cannot do.

If you really want to succeed, you must grasp and protect your own opportunities, and even try to seize others' opportunities.

(Conformity is the enemy of thought and the jailer of freedom.)

September 2, 1902

Dear John:

I appreciate your trust in me by informing me about your withdrawal from the board of directors of Citibank. Of course, I understand why you did this. You can no longer tolerate certain practices of your colleagues, let alone succumb to them.

However, whether your decision is wise or not has yet to be confirmed. The reason is simple. If you did not take the initiative to give up the position as the director of Citibank, but chose to stay there instead, you might have achieved more.

I know that being submissive is the enemy of thought and the jailer of freedom. However, for an ambitious person, maintaining the necessary obedience and patience is precisely a successful strategy that has been tried and tested. Looking back in the past, I have endured a lot, and I have gained a lot because of patience.

At the beginning of my business, due to the lack of funds, my partner, Mr. Clark, invited his former colleague, Mr. Gardner, to join in. I agreed to this, because with the addition of this rich man, it means that we can do what we want to do, as long as we have enough funds to do it.

However, to my surprise, with Clark's invitation of an investor, it brought me humiliation at the same time. They wanted to change the name of Clark-Rockefeller Company to Clark-Gardner Company. The reason for the change of company name was: Gardner was from a well-known family, his surname can attract more customers.

This was a reason that stabbed my dignity greatly! I was angry! I was also a partner, and Gardner only brought out his share of funds. Did this meant that being a nobleman gave him the rights to deprive me of my deserved status?! However, I tolerated it, and I told myself: You have to control yourself, you have to keep your mind calm, this is just the beginning, there is still a long way to go!

I pretended to be calm and told Clark, "It's nothing." In fact, this is a lie. Think about it, how can a person who suffer from injustice and a hurt self-esteem be so tolerant! However, I used rationality to extinguish the burning anger in my heart, because I knew it would bring me benefits.

Patience is not blind tolerance. You need to calmly consider the situation and know whether your decision will deviate from or harm your goals. It is not only disgraceful if I were to be angry with Clark, but more importantly, it will create rifts in our cooperation, cause me to be kicked out, and make me start all over again. Instead, unity can form a joint force, allowing our career to grow bigger, and at the same time, it will also allow my personal strength and interests to grow.

I know where I am going. After this, I continued to work tirelessly and enthusiastically as always. In the third year, I finally managed to exclude the extravagant Mr. Gardner out of the company, and the

Clark-Rockefeller brand was re-established! At that time people began to respect me as Mr. Rockefeller, and I became a rich man.

In my eyes, patience does not mean swallowing anger, neither is it humbling. Patience is a strategy, and it also trains your character. What it nurtures is a competitive heart. This is what I learned during my cooperation with Mr. Clark.

I admire equality and hate commanding orders from high ground. However, Mr. Clark always puts on a pretentious posture in front of me, which makes me very disgusted. He never seemed to pay attention to me but only regarded me as a short-sighted little clerk, and even belittled me for my inability to do nothing but bookkeeping and money management. Without him, I would be worthless. This is a blatant provocation, but I pretended to turn a deaf ear. I know that respecting myself is more important than anything else. However, I have been at war with him in my heart. I have told myself over and over again: surpass him, your strength will be the biggest humiliation to him, just like giving him the loudest slap across his face.

As you know, the Clark-Rockefeller Company has forever become a history. The Rockefeller-Andrews Company replaced it, and I got on the express train to become a billionaire. Only by being able to endure what people cannot bear, can you do what people cannot do.

Impulse is our worst enemy at any time. If patience can resolve conflicts that shouldn't occur, such patience will always be worthwhile; but if you stubbornly go your own way, not only will it fail to resolve the crisis, it will also bring even greater disasters. Mr. Andrews did not seem to understand this truth.

Mr. Andrews is a self-righteous man without a business acumen. He lacks the ambition to become a great businessman but has evil prejudices. It is no surprise that this kind of person will clash with me.

The conflict that led us to part ways was due to the company's dividends to shareholders. We did a good job that year and made a lot of money, but I did not want to let the shareholders take home all the money made by the company. I hoped to reinvest half of the proceeds in the company's operations. But Andrews firmly opposed the idea. This selfish guy wanted to divide the money we made, and even threatened me angrily that he did not want to continue working in the company. I cannot withstand any idea that prevented the company from becoming stronger. I can only lay the cards on the table and asked him to offer a price for his share of stocks. He said one million, and I said okay. I bought it over for one million the next day.

Andrews was so excited when he got the money. He thought he hit the jackpot and that the stock he held was not worth a million dollars. But he did not expect that I made 300,000 dollars soon after I changed hands. When the news got to him, he actually called me despicable. I did not want to earn a sordid reputation just because of the 300,000 dollars, so I sent someone to tell him that he could get it back at the original price. But Andrews, who was annoyed, rejected my kindness. In fact, what he refused was an opportunity to become a wealthy man in the United States. If he could keep his stocks that was worth one million up to this day, he would become a multimillionaire of course. But due to a moment of impulse, he lost the opportunity of a lifetime that he could never seize again.

John, there are too many people and things that require us to be patient in this world, and they entice us to be emotional. Therefore, you have to cultivate your ability to manage your emotions and control your emotions, and you should be careful not to be influenced by your emotions when making decisions, but to instead make decisions based on your needs and always know what you want. You also need to know that in the world of opportunity, there are not too many opportunities to fight for. If you really want to succeed, you must grasp and protect your own opportunities, and try to seize others' opportunities.

Remember, you must have patience in your daily life, it will bring you happiness, opportunities, and success.

Love,
Your Father

LETTER

27

God of Luck favours the Brave
Opportunity is in your choice.

If you do things right 51% of the time, then you will become a hero.

If you act like a winner, you are likely to do more of what a winner should do, thereby changing your "luck".

(The battle, sir, is not to the strong alone; it is to vigilant, the active, the brave.)

October 7, 1898

Dear John:

A few days ago your sister happily told me that she plunged into luck and said that the stocks in her hand are like slaves of her, who listen to her orders, and help her rake in a lot of money.

I think your sister may be happy and crazy now, but I don't want her to be overwhelmed by the money. I told her to be careful as luck might throw her into the field of failure.

Almost every successful person is warning the world: You cannot live by luck, especially when building a career. Interestingly, most people believe in luck, and I think they are mistaking chances to be luck. No opportunity, means no luck.

John, think about the lucky guys you know. You can almost be sure that they are not gentle, courteous, and frugal people, and can almost be certain that they always exude the brilliance of self-confidence and the attitude of everything, and even appear very bold. There is a problem of Chicken and Egg. Is it because of luck that the lucky ones show confidence and boldness, or is their "luck" the result of self-confidence and boldness? My answer is the latter.

"The god of luck favours the brave", is a motto that I have respected throughout my life. Victory does not necessarily belong to the strong, people who are highly vigilant, energetic, brave, and fearless will also win. Of course, some people believe that cautiousness is better than bravery. But bravery and boldness are more compelling, more popular, and more attractive than cautiousness, and cowardice cannot be compared to this.

I have never seen people who do not appreciate confident and decisive people. Everyone is a supporter of confident and decisive people. We expect such people to be leaders. The reason why we are attracted to them is that they are very attractive. Therefore, brave people are often more successful and it is easier for them to take on roles as leaders, presidents and commanders. Those who are promoted quickly belong to this kind of person.

Experience tells me that people who are bold and decisive can complete the best deal, attract the support of others, and form the most powerful alliance. Those who are timid and hesitant can hardly reap such benefits. Not only that, bold methods are also beneficial to them. People with confidence will turn their expectations into success. They will design all plans to pursue success in accordance with their expectations.

Of course, this does not guarantee absolute success, but it can naturally launch a vision for success. In other words, if you feel that you are a winner, you will behave like a winner; if you behave like a winner, you are likely to do more of what winners would do, thereby changing your "luck".

A true brave man is not an arrogant man, let alone a foolish man. The brave knows to use prediction and judgment, plan every step, and make every decision. This approach is just like what military strategists say, it will increase your strength, that is, possess a weapon that can immediately form a clear advantage to help you defeat your opponent. This reminds me of the bold decision to buy the Lima Oil field more than ten years ago.

Prior to this, the oil industry had not stopped fearing that crude oil would be exhausted. Even my assistants began to fear that they would not be able to profit from oil in the long run, hence quietly selling the company's stock; while some people even suggested that the company should exit the oil industry early and switch to other more stable industries, otherwise we will never be able to make a return. As a leader, in the face of pessimism, I should be hoping instead of lamenting. I told those in fear: God will give us everything.

I felt God's warm touch again when people discovered oil in Lima, Ohio. It's just that Lima's oil exudes a smell that cannot be removed by conventional methods, which deeply shook the confidence of many people who wanted to make a lot of money there. But I was strongly confident in Lima Oil field. I could foresee that once we monopolize Lima, we will have a powerful force over the oil market. The opportunity is here. If you let it slip away quietly, Rockefeller's name will be associated with pigs. I solemnly told the directors of the company: This is a once-in-a-lifetime opportunity, and it's time for us to invest our money in Lima!

It was a pity that my opinion was opposed by the timid.

Imposing on others is not in line with my personality. I was hoping that through peaceful discussions, everyone could finally agree with my opinions.

It was a long and fruitless wait. I was worried. We have built a giant oil refinery on a global scale. It was like a hungry baby who was greedy for its mother's milk. It needed to "*eat*" a steady stream of crude oil. But the oil fields in Pennsylvania were dying, and so were the other small oil fields. Production has begun to cut, and in the long run we will have to rely on Russian crude oil. It was almost certain that the Russians will use their control over oil fields to weaken our power, even defeat us completely, and drive us out of the European market. However, once we have Lima's oil resources, we will continue to be winners. Cannot wait any longer, it is time for me to act!

As I expected, conservatives still said "no" on the board. But I surrendered in the name of the opposition in a way that surprised them. I said: Gentlemen, if we do not want our huge ship to sink, we must guarantee our crude oil supply. Now, the oil hidden in Lima is beckoning to us, and it will bring us dazzling wealth. For the sake of God, please do not say that there is no market for the smelly liquid. I believe that everything God has given us has its value. I believe that science will clear our doubts. So, I decided to use my own money to make this investment and take the risk for two years. If it succeeds in two years, the company can return the money to me; if it fails, I will bear all the losses myself.

My determination and sincerity touched my biggest opponent, Mr. Pratt, as tears welled up in his eyes and excitedly said to me: "John, my heart is captured by you. Since you think we should do this, let's do it together! If you can take the risk, so can I!" The cooperative spirit of facing victories and losses together is also a spiritual pillar for our growth.

We succeeded. We made every effort to invest huge sums of money in Lima, and the rewards were even greater. We controlled the largest crude oil production base in the United States in our own hands. The success in Lima intensified our vitality and allowed us to dominate other unprecedented acquisition in the oil industry. As a result, like we expected, we became the most feared super fleet in the oil field and achieved unshakable dominance.

John, attitude helps create luck, and luck is in your choice. If you do it right 51% of the time, then you will become a hero.

This is my deepest experience with luck.

Love,
Your Father

LETTER

28

Only sincerely believing in yourself will find you a way

It is impossible to find the best way to do anything.

The best way to find the best idea is to have lots of ideas.

The greatest success is reserved for those who have the attitude that they can do things better.

(The best way to have a good idea is to have lots of ideas.)

December 4, 1903

Dear John:

I do not agree with your point of view, of letting Roger take on the heavy responsibility and face the music alone. In fact, with regards to this, I have worked hard, but the result was quite disappointing. My principle of employing people is that those who are entrusted with important tasks are those who can find ways to do things better. But Rogers is obviously not qualified, because he is a lazy person.

Before I started working with Roger, I tested him with a question. I said, "Mr. Roger, what do you think the government can do to abolish all prisons in thirty years?" He was confused when he heard it, and suspected that he had heard it wrong. After a while of silence, he began to refute me: "Dear Rockefeller Sir, do you mean to release all the murderers, robbers, and rapists? Do you know the consequences of doing this? If that's the case, we will not have peace. In anyway, there must be a prison."

I wanted to smash Rogers' monolithic head, and I reminded him: "Roger, you only said the reasons why the prison cannot be abolished. Now, try to believe that the prison can be abolished. Assuming it can be abolished, how should we proceed?"

"This is too hard for me, Mr. Rockefeller, I can't believe it, and it's hard for me to find a way to abolish it." This is Rogers's method – no way.

I cannot imagine how he will use all his talents to actively react when he is given a heavy responsibility, or when an opportunity or a crisis hit. I do not trust Roger; he will only turn hope into hopelessness.

Finding out a way to do things better is the guarantee of being able to complete anything. This does not require superhuman wisdom, the important thing is to believe that things can be done, and to have this belief. When we believe that something is impossible to do, our brain will find various reasons for us not to do it. However, when we believe—really believe that something can be done, our brain will help us find various ways.

Believing that something can be done will provide us with creative solutions and bring out our various creative abilities. On the contrary, not believing that things can be done successfully is tantamount to shutting down our wisdom in creative problem-solving, which will not only hinder our creative ability, but will also destroy our ideals. The so-called aspirational element turns out to be the foundation of creation and achievement, but that is it.

I hate my subordinates saying "impossible". "Impossible" is a term for failure. Once a person is dominated by the idea of "it is impossible", he can produce a series of ideas to prove that he is right. Roger made this mistake. He is a traditional thinker, and his mind is numb. His reason is: this has been practiced for a hundred years, so it must be a good way. It must be kept as it is, so why risk it. Change?

In fact, it can often be achieved only through thinking about the reasons diligently. "Ordinary people" always hate progress.

People believe that it is impossible to find the best way to do anything. The best way is to have as many creative ideas. Nothing grows on ice and snow. If we let traditional ideas freeze our hearts, new ideas will grow out of nowhere.

Traditional ideas are the number one enemy of creative planning. Traditional ideas will freeze our hearts and hinder us from developing the creative abilities we really need. Roger made such a mistake. He should be willing to accept all kinds of ideas, and discard the dregs of thoughts such as "unfeasible", "unable", "useless", "that's stupid", etc.; he should also have an experimental spirit to be brave enough to try new things, which will expand his abilities and prepare him for greater responsibilities. At the same time, he must take the initiative to move forward, instead of thinking – "this is usually the way I do this, so here I also want to use this method", but instead think of – Is there any way to do better than our usual method?

It is impossible for various plans to achieve absolute perfection, which means that all things can be improved endlessly. I know this well, so I often look for better methods. I do not ask myself: Can I do better? I know I can do it, so I ask: How can I do better?

The best way to find the perfect idea is to have many ideas. I will continue to set higher standards for myself and others, and constantly seek various ways to improve efficiency, get more rewards at a lower cost, and do more things with less energy. Because I know that the greatest success is those who have the attitude that I can do things better.

To develop an attitude that I can do better, we need to cultivate, and to reflect every day: How can I do better today? How can I motivate employees today? What special services can I provide for the company? How can I make my work more efficient? This exercise is simple, but very useful. You can try it; I believe you will find countless creative ways to win greater success.

Our mentality determines our ability. If we think we can do this much, we can really do that much. If we truly believe that we can do more, we can think creatively about various methods.

It is very stupid to refuse new challenges. We have to focus on how we can do more. In this way, many creative answers will come unexpectedly. For example, to improve the current work plan, to deal with routine work shortcuts, or to accomplish trivial matters. In other words, most of the methods that enable us to do more will appear at this time.

John, you can talk to Roger. I hope he can change. It is then he will have a better life.

Love,
Your Father

LETTER
29

The ending is the beginning
It is better to be a good enemy.

The person who first discovers the opponent's weakness and strikes hardly is often the winner.

Most people fail, not because they make mistakes, but because they are not fully committed.

(I believe it to be an invariable rule that competitors of genius are succeeded by warriors.)

August 31, 1908

Dear John:

Mr. Andrew Carnegie accepted an interview with reporters again. I have never figured out why he always likes to appear the newspapers, I guess he must be suffering from amnesiophobia, lest people ignore his existence.

But I still appreciate this guy who often competes with me, because he is diligent and ambitious, like a tireless iron man, always regarding moving forward as his first, second, and third most important thing; maybe because of this, when asked about the secret of his success, he would tell reporters that the end is just the beginning.

It is unbelievable, how can this blacksmith say such brilliant words. I believe that this short sentence which consists of only three words will soon be broadcasted far away, and Mr. Carnegie will hold the title of a business philosopher. In fact, he deserves to be praised by people like this. Doesn't the fact that he is able to condense his successful life into a short sentence show the great wisdom of this business mogul?

However, Mr. Carnegie only gave a successful formula for success, but did not give the calculation process. It seems that this guy just cannot change his selfish nature, and he is always afraid that others will see the secret behind his success. I want to try to solve the formula of the blacksmith, but do not tell it to others; otherwise, for leaking out his secret, he will not only send me whiskey during Christmas, but he will also definitely send cigars. He knows that I do not drink alcohol, and he knows that I am an anti-smoker, this funny guy.

"The end is just the beginning." In my opinion, this blacksmith is trying to show that success is a process of continuous reproduction, just like a prolific cow. When it gives birth to a calf, it immediately becomes pregnant with another. Back and forth, endlessly. The end is the last stop of a journey and the beginning of a new dream. Every great successful person builds himself up with small successes. They celebrate the realization of their dreams with the ending and at the same time, mark the beginning of their new dreams. This is the quality of every person who has accomplished great achievements.

But how do we start a new dream? Mr. Carnegie "had forgotten" to talk about it, and this is precisely the key in determining whether we can expect a smooth journey to the last stop, and it is also the key to starting the next new dream. In fact, the answer is very simple, that is, from the beginning you have to do everything possible in order to get an advantage. My experience tells me that there are three strategies that give me an advantage.

The first strategy: Make up your mind from the beginning and pay attention to the competition and the resources of competitors. This means that I have to pay attention to what my competitors and I have, and it also means that I have to understand the fundamentals of reducing opportunities. When starting a new business, you should not take preliminary actions until you understand the overall situation. The first step to success is to understand where and how many resources are needed to achieve your goal.

From the very beginning, I tried to predict what opportunities would appear, and when it appeared, I would pounce on it like a lion. And I also know that it is better to be a good enemy, many people always like to pursue the best things that comes up and give up the good things. This is not a smart strategy, because good always beats bad. The reality is that ideal opportunities rarely come to the door, but there are often many unsatisfactory ones. However, although good opportunities have shortcomings, they are definitely far better than no opportunities at all.

The second strategy: research and review the opponent's situation, and then make good use of this knowledge to form your advantages. Understanding the strengths, weaknesses, style of doing things, and personality traits of my opponents always gives me an advantage in the competition. Of course, I also need to know who I am. I used this strategy to make Mr. Carnegie, the inventor of "the end is just the beginning", concede defeat.

Mr. Carnegie is a well-deserved steel magnate and challenging him is like challenging death. But his weakness can help his opponent a lot. He is stubborn. Maybe his wallet is too big. He always likes to look down and underestimate others. He did not pay any attention to me, stupidly thinking that the oil industry was where I belonged, and he stubbornly believed that only stupid people would go to the mining line, because he thought ore was inexhaustible and its price was too low.

Therefore, when I invested in the mining industry, he always ridiculed me, saying that I knew nothing about the steel industry and was the most failed investor in the United States. In fact, Carnegie is a man who only sees the mountainside but not the top of the mountain. He does not know that price is not sacred. The important thing is value. If he can't control the mining industry, his proud steel mills can only be moved to become a pile of scrap iron.

When others do not regard you as an opponent, it is when you earn the most capital for future competition. Therefore, from the beginning, I was confident that I will invest boldly and fully. Impulse is better than prudence. Soon the proud blacksmith discovered that the "man who is known as the worst investor in the world" now has control over the iron mining industry and became the largest iron ore producer in the United States, gaining a dominant position and wanting to fight with him. He could not be at ease and begged to make peace.

In a competition, the person who first discovers the opponent's weakness and strikes hard is often the winner.

The third strategy: You must have the right mindset. From the beginning, you must make up your mind to pursue victory, which means that you must act positively and ruthlessly under moral constraints, because this attitude comes directly from cruel and ruthless goals.

Since you are determined to pursue victory, you must go all out. Only by going all out can there be glorious achievements. This is especially true when the competition begins. To put it nicely, this is an effort to gain an early advantage, hoping to establish an exclusive position, but to put it bluntly, putting in effort is equal to depriving others of a chance. At the same time, we have to be positive and brave, and have the courage to "swallow whales". I believe that talented competitors are always borne by the warriors. This is a time-honoured law.

In the "New Testament", the apostle Paul said: "There is faith, hope, and love that are always present today. The biggest of these three is love." At the beginning of every new dream, the most important thing is the determination to pursue victory. Not having the right attitude of wanting to pursue victory, makes factors such as paying attention to the situation of the competition and understanding the opponent redundant. Gaining knowledge, maintaining control, and evaluating competition are what builds your confidence and will assist you in achieving the highest goal of victory.

Look at those who fail, and you will find that most people fail not because they make mistakes, but because they are not fully committed, and the same goes for companies.

John, do not forget Mr. Carnegie's famous saying, "The end is just the beginning", and of course, my three strategies.

Oh, I am not rescuing a planner who does not need to be rescued.

Love,
Your Father

LETTER
30

Do not let the villain hold you back

A wise man will never sit down and mourn over fate.

Those who say you cannot do it are those who cannot succeed.

You cannot afford all the extra burdens accumulated by greed and loss.

(Let me embrace thee, sour adversity, for wise men say it's the wisest course.)

May 11, 1902

Dear John:

I think you have noticed that some of your thoughts and concepts are changing because of your friend. I certainly do not object to your expansion of your social circle, as it can increase your interest in life, expand your area of life, or even help you find a confidant or help you achieve your ideals in life. But some people are obviously not worth-associating with, for example, those who are petty and trivial.

Since I was young, I have refused to associate with two kinds of people.

The first type of people is those who completely surrender and are contented with the status quo. They are convinced that they are inadequate and believe that creative achievements are only the patent that belongs to the lucky ones. They do not have this blessing. This kind of person is willing to guard a very secure but ordinary position, year after year in a muddle-headed manner. They also know that they need a more challenging job in order to continue to develop and grow, but because of countless resistances, they are convinced that they are not suitable for doing big things.

A wise man will never sit down and mourn over fate. But this kind of people will only lament over their bad destiny, but they will never appreciate themselves and regard themselves as important and valuable people. They have already lost the feeling of putting in their utmost effort and the ability to self-encourage, and instead let negativity occupy their heart.

The second type of people are those who cannot complete challenges. They used to yearn for accomplishments and they also made great preparations and plans for their work. But after a few years or even decades, as work resistance gradually increase, when hard work is required to attain higher levels, they will feel that it is not worth continuing so they give up on their efforts and themselves.

They will ridicule themselves: "We earn more than ordinary people, and our lives are better than ordinary people. Why are we still dissatisfied and want to take risks?" In fact, such people already have a sense of fear. They are afraid of failure, afraid that everyone will disagree with them, afraid of an accident, and afraid of losing what they already have. They are not satisfied, but they have surrendered. Some people of this kind are very talented, but because they dare not take risks again, they are willing to spend their life in peace.

These two kinds of people share a common, yet toxic thought and it is highly infectious. This thought is also known as negativity.

I have always thought that a person's personality and ambitions, current status and positions are related to who they associate themselves with. If he often associates with negative people, he himself will become negative. If he associates closely with insignificant people, he will have many petty habits. On the other hand, if he is constantly influenced by important people, it will improve his ideological level; frequent contact with successful people with ambitions will also enable him to develop the ambitions and actions needed to succeed.

I like to be friends with those who never give in. A wise man said it well: I want to challenge the repulsive adversity, because a wise man told me that that is the wisest direction to success. It is just that there are very few such people.

This kind of person will never allow pessimism to influence anything, and will never succumb to all kinds of resistance, let alone believe that they can only spend their lives in a muddle-headed manner. The purpose of their lives is to achieve success. Such people are very optimistic, because they must fulfil their wishes. Such people can easily become the best in any fields. They can truly enjoy life and truly understand the value of life. They all look forward to every new day and new interactions with others because they regard these as enriching life experiences, so they enthusiastically accept it.

I believe everyone wants to be included in this category, because only these people can succeed, and only these people can really do things and get the results they expect.

Unfortunately, negative people can be seen everywhere, and many, many people cannot escape the siege of negativity.

The people around us are not the same, some are passive and conservative, some are aggressive. Some of the people I have worked with, some people just want to make a living, some are ambitious and want to perform better. They also understand that before becoming a big man, you must be a good follower.

To be successful, one must avoid falling into various traps or snares. In any place, there are people who know they cannot succeed but they insist on blocking your way up and preventing you from attaining higher levels. Many people are ridiculed or even intimidated because of their ambitions. Others are very jealous. Seeing you work hard and strive to outperform them will make them try their best to fool you and make you embarrassed.

We cannot prevent others from becoming boring negative people, but we cannot be influenced by them and lower our level of thinking. You will want them to slip past naturally, just like the water behind a mallard. People who always follow their thoughts and move forward actively will grow and progress with them.

You can indeed do this, as long as your mind is sane, you can do it, and you'd better do it.

Some negative people have a very good heart, and there are other negative people who do not want to work hard, but also want to drag others into the water. They have nothing so they want to make others achieve nothing. Remember, John, people who say you cannot do it are people who cannot succeed, that is, his personal achievements are at best ordinary. Therefore, the opinion of such a person is harmful to you.

You have to take precautions against those who say you can't do it. You can only treat their warnings as a challenge to prove that you can do it. You have to take special precautions against negative people from sabotaging your plan to succeed. Such people can be seen everywhere. They seem to be dedicated to sabotaging the progress and efforts of others. Be careful, pay more attention to those negative people, and do not let them ruin your plans to succeed. Do not let those with negative thinking and narrow judgement hinder your progress. Those who are jealous and like to gloat just want to watch you fall, do not give them a chance.

When you have any difficulties, it is wise to find people of top quality to help you. Asking a loser for advice is as ridiculous as asking a quack to treat a terminal illness. Your future is very important. Do not ask for advice from a yenta, because this kind of person has no prospects in their lives.

You have to pay attention to your environment. Just as food supplies the body, mental activity will also nourish your mental health. Make your environment serve your work, not drag you down. Do not let those resistance, that is, people who pull you on your hind legs, make you sluggish. The way to let the environment help you succeed is to get closer to the positive and successful people and to interact less with the negative people.

Everything must be done perfectly. You cannot afford all the extra burdens accumulated from greed and loss.

Love,
Your Father

LETTER

31

Be Teleological

Loyalty is the beginning of willingness to serve.

The road to hell is paved with kindness.

Purpose is the basis of my leadership, and *purpose* is everything.

(A human can alter his life by altering his attitude, and if you think you can do it, you're right.)

May 11, 1902

Dear John:

It is your glory and my glory that you are at the core of Standard Oil. However, you need to know that when you are enjoying this glory, you undoubtedly have to shoulder the responsibilities that accompany it. Otherwise, you will be ashamed of this glory, and will disappoint everyone's hope and trust in you. Do not forget that you are the backbone of Standard Oil Company. The ultimate success or failure of our business is closely related to you. You should have higher demands for yourself when it comes to strength and sacrifice.

Frankly speaking, if you want to do a good job in that position, and let everyone recognize you and admire you, you still need to learn a lot. Now, you need to think about a question: whether you can successfully master this role yourself.

Every leader is an ambassador of hope and a teacher for his subordinates on the unavoidable thorny road ahead. But not being let down is difficult. As a leader, no matter who you are, you will face many problems, such as mountains of work, mountains of information, sudden changes, endless requests from top management, investors and customers, and employees who are difficult to train. Challenges that are always changing can make you exhausted, feel frustrated, fearful, anxious, and overwhelmed, which might shatter your dreams of achieving business and personal success.

However, sometimes it is easier to become an excellent leader full of confidence and vitality than to become a leader who has lost vitality and is struggling and helpless, provided that he needs to know how to make his subordinates willing to give up their lives. Take note, it is willing, not chased.

As the leader of Standard Oil Company, I enjoy both authority and pleasure, because I know that finding someone who can guarantee the completion of the task is equivalent to creating time for myself. In other words, it will not only make me energetic, but also more importantly it will give me more time to think about how to make more money for the company.

There is an attitude issue here. Actions are driven by attitudes. The attitude we choose determines what behaviour we want to take. As for the results, it will soon be apparent to us. People can change their lives by changing their attitudes. If you believe that you can change your attitude you can change it.

Smart people always choose the attitude that is best for them. People who know the art of leadership will always ask themselves: What kind of attitude can help them achieve the results they really want? Is it an inspiring attitude? Or is it sympathetic? They will never choose a cold or hostile attitude.

If you think of yourself as a supreme, desperate monarch, you are likely to become the next King Louis XVI. As far as I am concerned, I never dominate, create conflicts, or put too much pressure on myself. Instead, I have the habit of giving subordinates trust, boosting their morales, and in turn, achieving the business achievements I expect. This habit will help me achieve the purpose I want by using subordinates. The way of doing this is very simple, and that is to know how to use the power of setting goals.

I am a teleologist. I never exaggerate the function of having a goal like some people do, but I attach great importance to its function. In my opinion, purpose is the driving force behind our potential, and it is the power that governs everything. It can affect our behaviour and inspire us to create the means to achieve our goals. A clear and decisive purpose will allow us to focus on the chosen direction and allow us to try our best to achieve the goal.

My experience tells me that the tasks a person accomplishes, and his ultimate performance are closely related to the nature and power of his purpose and have almost nothing to do with what he does for his goal. Think about it, there is no game of golf that can be completed in one stroke. You need to complete the holes one by one. The goal of each stroke is to get as close to the hole as possible.

Having a purpose is the basis of my leadership, and it is everything. I am accustomed to establishing goals before doing anything, and every day I have to set goals, countless goals, such as the purpose of talking with partners, the purpose of convening meetings, the purpose of making plans, and so on. Before doing something, I will also review the purpose that I have set. Usually when I arrive at the company, I have already prepared everything. Therefore, I have never "swallowed" voices such as "I can't help it", "I don't care anymore", "There is no hope anymore" in my heart. The purpose that I establish every day has offset these failures.

If you are unable to actively establish your own goals, you will passively or unconsciously choose other goals. As a result, you may lose control of the overall situation. At the same time, you will be subjected to people or events that might distract you or disturb you.

It is like loosening a yacht from the dock and forgetting to start the motor. You will follow the currents, and sea breeze, currents or other ships that might collide into you and cause you to sink to the bottom of the sea at any time. Maybe something good is waiting for you on the other side, but unless a miracle occurs, you will not be able to reach the other side smoothly. Establishing a purpose is like turning on the engine of a yacht, which can propel you towards the path you choose. Purpose can add direction and strength to human efforts.

However, establishing a purpose only brings you to the midst of the route to becoming a teleologist, and you have to complete the other half of the journey. You need to unreservedly state your purpose to your subordinates – your personal intentions, motives and inner strategic plans. For everyone who needs to understand what I want to achieve, I will explain my purpose to them. In every meeting, report or at the beginning of the matter, I will first express my motivation, thoughts, and expectations.

The benefits of this will surprise you. It not only enables your subordinates to know your purpose and brings them the right direction to move forward, but most importantly, when you have the courage to be honest about your purpose, you will gain emotional loyalty. Know that loyalty is the beginning of willingness to serve.

Outstanding leaders are good at using two invisible forces: trust and respect. When you honestly stated your purpose, you also deliver this message: "Because I have enough trust in you, I am willing to confess to you." It will open the door for people to trust you, and what you embrace is not only the ability of your subordinates, but also the priceless loyalty from them – the loyalty that must be gathered to help you. Trusting others and making others trust myself are the important reasons for my achievements in life.

Exposing your purpose can better avoid unhelpful inferences. If you do not tell your subordinates about your purpose, they will spend time guessing what it is based on the clues they can collect, and this information is easily distorted. Only when they do not need to interpret your motives, will the morale and ability of subordinates have a chance to be improved. Therefore, it seems more advantageous to treat subordinates as "fools."

The power expressed by purpose is irreplaceable. What it conveys is not only a statement, but also the leader's courageous and resolute oath for personal behaviour. The purpose of resolute will and absolute tenacity can often inspire and encourage subordinates, so that they can deliver more outstanding performance in the future work.

The mission of a leader is to discover problems and solving problems depends on subordinates. How to mobilize subordinates and fulfil their duties is the first priority for leaders. I think that by showing your purpose and treating everyone with enthusiasm, you can achieve what you want.

Purpose is like a diamond: if it is to be valuable, it must be real. An insincere purpose confession will only be bad. If one abuses the power of purpose, he will only destroy mutual trust and lose the trust of others. This is the risk of expressing purpose.

John, the road to hell is paved with kindness. Unless you are fully prepared, this sentence is likely to come true.

Love,
Your Father

LETTER

32

Avoid Blaming and giving excuses

Blaming is the number one enemy in destroying a leadership.

Self-blame is one of the most insidious and cunning traps.

The stronger you are, the lesser the influence others will have.

(Action springs not from thought, but from a readiness for responsibility.)

July 24, 1910

Dear John:

If I say Mr. Andrew Carnegie, who has always been unwilling to be outdone and always thought he is the richest man in the world, came to visit me and consulted me on a very serious question., Would you be surprised? In fact, that great blacksmith did just that.

Two days ago, Mr. Carnegie came to our Kikwit. Perhaps it was my smile, the relaxed atmosphere while we were conversing, that melted Mr. Carnegie's steely self-esteem, as he put his ego aside and asked:

"John, I know, you lead a group of very capable people. But I do not think their talents are extraordinary, but what puzzles me is that they seem to be invincible and can always easily defeat your competitors. I want to know what magic you have done to make them have that kind of spirit. Is it the power of money?"

I told him that the power of money is certainly not to be underestimated, but the power of responsibility is even greater. Sometimes actions do not come from ideas, but from taking responsibility. Everyone at Standard Oil Company has a sense of responsibility, and they all know "What is my responsibility? What can I do to make things better?" But I never talk about responsibilities or obligations. I just create a sense of responsibility in the company through my leadership.

I thought this topic should be over at this point, but my answer obviously stimulated Mr. Carnegie's curiosity. He asked me seriously: "John, can you tell me how you did it?"

Seeing Mr. Carnegie's humble expression, I could not refuse, I had to tell the truth. I told him that if we want to survive forever, our leadership style means we have to refuse blaming anyone or anything for any reason. The habit of blaming is like a swamp. Once you stumble and fall into it, you will lose your footing and direction, you will become unable to move and then fall into the predicament of hatred and frustration. There is only one result: losing the respect and support of your subordinates. Once you fall into this field, you are like a king who has handed over the crown to others, unable to dominate anything anymore.

I know that blaming is the number one enemy that destroys leadership. I also know that in this world, there is no eternal victorious general. No matter who it is, they will encounter setbacks and failures. Therefore, when a problem arises, I will not feel resentful or dissatisfied. I will just think how can the situation get better? What actions can be taken to solve or repair the situation? Or how can we actively choose to move towards higher productivity and satisfaction.

Of course, I will not let myself go. When something bad happens to us, I will stop and ask myself a question: "What are my responsibilities?" Going back to the original point, by fully and honestly assessing my role, I can avoid spying on what others have done, or asking other people to change something and doing other meaningless actions. In fact, only by focusing on myself can I reclaim the crown that I inadvertently gave up.

However, analysing "what are my responsibilities" does not mean self-blame. Self-blame is one of the most insidious and cunning traps. Self-blaming such as "That was a stupid mistake!" will only make me fall into the same trap of resentment and dissatisfaction as any other accusations will. In fact, "what are my responsibilities" is a step with strong analytical power and self-affirmation. When I know that the real problem is not what they should do, but what I should do, I will not complain about myself, which will only make yourself stronger. The stronger you are, the smaller the influence of others will be. It seems that this is not a bad thing.

If I can treat every obstacle as an opportunity to understand myself, rather than care about what others have done to me, then I can find a way out of the face of adversities.

Of course, I never see myself as a saviour, nor do I have a mentality of a saviour. I will ask myself: In what ways should I be responsible for myself? I also asked myself: In what aspects are my subordinates responsible for? The job of a leader is not omniscient, or to assume full responsibility. If I regard myself as a brave messenger of justice, ready to save the world, I will only plunge myself into a crisis of leadership. A large part of my responsibilities is to make others accountable for their own responsibilities. If an employee does not care about things that concern his own interests, I do not believe that such an employee will have a strong desire to do a good job, then he should leave and serve others.

The kind of pressure that responsibility gives can make people unconsciously excited. Nothing can stimulate and strengthen the ability to do things like a sense of personal responsibility, and by entrusting the heavy responsibilities to my subordinates and letting them understand that I fully trust them is undoubtedly the greatest help to them. Therefore, I will not take the responsibilities that my subordinates must and can bear.

I not only rely on demonstration to create a responsible atmosphere and atmosphere for the company, my subordinates all know my basic principle: There is no blame or excuses at Standard Oil! This is the philosophy I insist on, everyone knows that. I will not punish them for making mistakes, but I will never tolerate irresponsible behaviour. Our belief is to be thoroughly implemented in the company's culture. Our motto is that support, encouragement, and respect will be wholeheartedly accepted and double praised. Only making excuses without providing solutions is intolerable in Standard Oil.

We seldom make any mistakes because my door is always open to my subordinates. They can offer opinions or simply complain, but in a responsible way. This result will make us trust each other, because we understand that everything needs to be discussed under the sun.

Mr. Carnegie is an excellent old student. He did not let me waste time. When I ended this topic, he said: "Amidst complaints, even the excellent employees can become mobs!" He is so smart.

John, almost all people have the defensive psychology of shirking real responsibility, so that the phenomenon of appointing committee responsibility can be seen everywhere. But it is harmful. The way to avoid defence is to start listening.

The biggest challenge for leaders is how to create an environment in which people feel that being open is more comfortable than hiding the truth. Proactively invite others to state their thoughts and encourage them to speak out with words such as "Say a little more" or "I really want to hear your opinion." Contrary to what most people believe, in a dialogue, the listener is the one who has the power, not the declarant.

Is this unbelievable? Think about it, the tone, focus, and content of the speaker actually depends on the way you listen. Imagine the difference between a person who is hostile and aggressive, and a person who is engrossed in you. When you simply listen to other people, you lower your defences. You will get these benefits: You will have a more thorough understanding of the underlying issues as compared to behind that of offensive or angry language. You can get more information, and this information can change your assumptions about the ins and outs of the entire event. You will have more time to organize your thoughts.

The presenter will feel that you value their point of view. The most exciting thing is that when you listen attentively, the original presenter will be more willing to listen to your opinions.

Listening truthfully is not defensive. Even if you do not like this information, you should listen to it instead of responding immediately. Listening attentively is less like a technique, it is more like an attitude. A skier spends 100% of his attention when encountering obstacles, and he will never be distracted to think about what he wants to say to his partner later. In the same way, as an active listener, you give 100% of your attention to another person, and you will not want to blurt out what you think. In this way, you get rid of preconceived notions and open your mind to create a more meaningful and effective dialogue.

For a long time, we have shaped our lives and lives have also shaped ourselves. This process will continue, and we will ultimately be responsible for our choices. Just as "purpose" determines your direction, refusal to blame will build a road to achieve your goals.

Love,
Your Father

LETTER

33

Making good use of everyone's wisdom

Do not use your own likes and dislikes as the criteria for selecting talents.

Being loyal to yourself will help you to win one of the greatest battles in your life.

The person who can create value the most is the person who devotes himself completely to his favourite activities.

(The most perfect human being is the one who most thoroughly addresses himself to the activity of his best powers.)

November 17, 1912

Dear John:

Receiving your letter is very exciting to me, because you understand my philosophy which always helps me to succeed in my career: do what you like to do, and leave other things to the people who like to do it.

For me, doing what I love is an unquestionable conclusion. It always reminds me that in order to lead my subordinates to complete tasks well, we must not rely on certain management skills, but adopt a more macroscopic and effective leadership style.

Specifically, it is not to let the subordinates stick to rigid and standardized work positions, but to find ways to use each person's strengths and induce them to pour enthusiasm into their work to achieve excellent productivity. This is my way to victory.

When I was studying, I remembered this sentence: "The most perfect person is the one who thoroughly devotes himself to the activity he is best at." Later, after I reformed it, I changed it into a management philosophy: The person who is most able to create value is the one who is completely devoted to his favourite activities.

I have said that everyone has the instinct to be loyal to themselves and have desires to be who they want to be, and the way they achieve loyalty is to do what they like to do. Unfortunately, many managers do not treat employees loyally, which results in lower productivity.

In fact, this is easy to understand. If you don't devote time to the things you love, you will never feel self-satisfied; if you don't have self-satisfaction, you will lose the passion for life; if you lose the passion for life , You will lose the motivation of life. Counting on a person who has lost the motivation to do a job well is like counting on a clock that has stopped to tell the time accurately. It is ridiculous.

Therefore, I never forget to give my subordinates the opportunity to be loyal to themselves – to ignite their enthusiasm and to maximize their special talents, and what I gain from it is precisely the wealth and achievement. Being loyal to yourself will win one of the greatest battles in your life. Who will miss this opportunity?

If you want to successfully use the enthusiasm of your subordinates, you must know that the responsibility of the leader is not to tap the weaknesses of the subordinates, but to pay attention to the strengths and talents of the subordinates, and let these advantages be fully utilized. I do not have the habit of picking the most vulnerable characteristics of my subordinates, but I always look for the strongest part of them so that their talents can be fully utilized in the challenges and needs of the work. For example, I reused Mr. Archibald.

Unlike some people, I do not use my likes and dislikes as the criteria for selecting talents first. I do not look at what signs are attached to them, what I like is their ability that they show when working. I like my preferences, but I prefer efficiency.

Archibald is by no means a perfect person. He is addicted to alcohol, but I am a prohibitionist of alcohol. However, Archibald has an extraordinary leadership talent and potentials. He is quick-witted, optimistic, and humorous. His outstanding eloquence, bold and combative character are undoubtedly the guarantee of winning in fierce competition, so after becoming a partner from an opponent, I have always been interested in him, and I kept entrusting him with important tasks until he was promoted to take over my position.

He has proven that he is a talented leader and his career is so special. If he is not affected by bad habits, his grades will be even more brilliant.

My purpose is to find the value that I value in every subordinate, not the shortcomings that I do not like. I find out what each employee is worthy of attention and strengths, and I am committed to turning the strengths of the employees into outstanding talents without trying to correct their shortcomings. Therefore, I always have subordinates who are capable and willing to contribute.

John, no one is omnipotent. Now, you are a manager, your achievements depend on the exertion of your leadership ability and your subordinates' ability to do things. You need to know that there are many places where you can pick on your subordinates, but you have to focus on discovering the potential strengths of each person, pay attention to their outstanding performance in every detail, and their insistence on perfectionism in order to do things well. This is where your leadership strength lies.

One person cannot dominate a team. I do not deny the great role of leaders, but on the whole, victory depends on the team. Any honour I get depends on the strength of the team, and not myself alone. Only when everyone works hard can they believe and expect miracles.

Good luck, my son!

Love,
Your Father

LETTER
34

Always think strategically
We have to be brave when there are no options, and resolutely find a way out.

The best way to find the perfect idea, is to have many ideas.

Planners who simply manipulate methods only benefit strategic thinkers.

(Become a possibilitarian, always see them, for they're always there.)

October 14, 1904

Dear John:

Dr. Hamilton has gotten rounder. It seems that golf cannot restrain his waist from expanding, he can only use other exercises reduce fat. Unfortunately, the exercise that can prevent him from gaining weight has not yet been invented, and he is suffering. However, he can always bring us happiness, by using all kinds of weird stories in his mind.

Today, Dr. Hamilton entertained us again with a story of a fisherman and an angler. Perhaps the doctor seemed very proud to see us all laughing. He smiled and shut me off: "Mr. Rockefeller, do you want to be a fisherman or an angler?"

I told him that if I became an angler, maybe I would not be qualified to play golf with him, because I would be relying on effective behavioural strategies to create business benefits, and the angler's behaviour cannot guarantee my success.

Of course, no angler is so stupid that he just throws down the bait without thinking, planning, and deciding in advance: what kind of fish to catch, what kind of bait to use, where to throw the fishing line, and then wait for the big fish to take the bait. As far as the fishing form is concerned, they have done nothing wrong, but no one knows whether the result is what they want.

Maybe it takes a while for them to catch a fish, maybe they cannot catch a single fish, and the fish they dream of may never be caught. Because they are too obsessed with their own methods, even though they are very clear about their goals, their methods limit the possibility of success – except where the fishing line can reach, their fishing range is equal to zero. However, if they can fish with a net like a fisherman, it will expand the fishing range, and the abundance of fish will give them many choices and eventually catch the fish they want.

I told Mr. Hamilton and my golf friends that I am not a stubborn, step-by-step angler who solves problems in a simple way. I am a fisherman who can create a variety of choices until the fish that can create the most commercial benefits. They all laughed and said that I had leaked the secret of making money.

John, no matter what you do, the best way to find the perfect idea is to have a lot of ideas. Before making the best decision, I will devote myself to look for creative and effective options, consider a variety of possibilities, and actively try various options, and then focus on the best option.

This is why I can always catch the big fish I want. Of course, in the process of implementing the plan, I will maintain an open strategy, adapt to the situation, and constantly adjust or revise my plan; therefore, even if the plan is not going well, I will not panic, and I can always respond calmly.

Many people think that I have extraordinary abilities, and I am a leader full of efficiency and ability to act. If this is the case, I think you can also get such praise, but you need to refrain from the urge to find simple, one-way solutions. Be willing to try various possible ways to achieve your goals, and have the patience to act in the face of difficulties, courage and resourcefulness, as well as the perseverance of never letting go without reaching the goal.

Planners who simply manipulate means only benefit the strategists. As the president, I only set clear directions or strategies for my subordinates, but I will not limit myself to an overly rigid action plan. On the contrary, I will continue to explore the various possibilities that can implement the strategy.

Many people insist that the key to success lies in a solid strategic plan, and this plan must be backed by concrete, measurable, achievable, and practical action goals. I admit that this is very important, but it has fatal flaws. The plan emphasizes the standard of judgment and the pre-determined results, and what people adopt is also a fixed method that believes that the goal can be achieved. Since these programs are based on known methods that are expected to achieve the goal, we have in fact limited the scope before we start.

Although the plan may seem seamless when we first drafted the plan, the situation may have changed before the plan was finalized. That is to say, not only the market situation has long changed, but the customers have changed, and even the factors that support the plan. Resources have also changed. It is no wonder that these costly, time-consuming, and labour-intensive strategies only have very few parts that can be implemented.

How to deal with this situation? Whether we are drawing up a plan for a company or a single department, we must confirm that what we are drawing up is a strategy, not a means. The essence of strategy is flexibility, long-term, multi-faceted, and large-scale. They emphasize results such as how to grow or expand profits, rather than a measurable goal. At the same time, the strategy provides a general direction, not the only way to achieve success.

To become an outstanding leader, we must make ourselves a strategic thinker, not just a designer of means. We also have to avoid confining ourselves to the established plans. Our motto will still to be focused, but also being flexible. We focus on the process of exploration. In every minute of every day, we can create possible directions that help achieve long-term goals.

We will not adhere to just three or five ways to achieve remote goals. Instead, we must always be able to discover opportunities for profit—whether in conversations with opponents or brainstorming meetings with subordinates.

In order to stay away from the storm of crisis, we must constantly formulate new strategies while adjusting the old plans. While responding to the daily changes in the business environment, we must also revise the long-term process based on changes in the situation. In this way, not only can we maintain a flexibility in the short term, and in the long run, we also have a clear concept of a flexible ideal goal that can meet the latest economic environment. We can put stale strategic plans on the shelf and move forward to a vibrant environment with energy and hope.

You have to be a hopeful person. No matter how bad the situation looks or how bad it actually is, please keep your eyes open to find the infinite hope in it – never give up searching, because hope will always exist.

I believe that all leaders have the obligation to provide hope, not only for themselves, but also guide their employees onto a broad road. Think back to the time in your life when you felt the most hopeless. It might be because you felt that you had nowhere to go or believed that you had no other choice. You were trapped, abandoned, and could not find a way out.

There is only one way to overcome despair, and that is to continue to create possibilities to overcome obstacles. Simply put, hope comes from believing that there are alternatives.

Outstanding leaders have the ability to cope with specific business situations, manoeuvre plans to create new markets, tips for coping with crises, and blueprints for career development for themselves and their employees. When the situation seems to have fallen to the bottom and is irretrievable, they are like brave wrestlers, even if they are suppressed by their opponents and it is difficult to get out, they will never give up any opportunity to turn over.

With their talents, flexibility, and adaptable wisdom, they cleverly find gaps and escape danger. They have no choice but to make a way out.

If you can be creative at the beginning, you can avoid endless exhaustion, frustration, and pain.

When things seem to have reached the point of despair, if we still hold on to endless hope, we will be able to surpass the boundaries set by ourselves and provide subordinates with new choices. Therefore, we must have the courage to find a way out of no choices.

Love,
Your Father

LETTER

35

Putting your subordinates first
Always put the employees who worked for me first.

Blindly asking and not willing to pay, will eventually face a day of exhaustion.

Give people the respect they deserve, and they can fully realize their potential.

(Everyone has an invisible sign hanging from his neck saying: Make me feel important!)

September 19, 1925

Dear John:

Imagine a scene like this: a conductor of a symphony orchestra, ready to let the audience who bought tickets enjoy a spectacular performance, but he turned to face the audience, leaving the musicians behind to battle alone and perform. What would happen?

Yes! This is destined to be the worst concert ever. Because the conductor did not attach any importance to the, and the latter will "thank" him with passive laziness and mess up everything.

Every employer is like a conductor of an orchestra. He dreams of inspiring and mobilizing the strength of all employees to make as many contributions as possible, helping him play the gorgeous music that makes money, and letting him earn much more money. However, for many employers, this is destined to be an unattainable dream, because they are like that stupid commander, forgetting to treat employees well, so that they easily close the door to which employees are willing to put in effort.

Like them, I expect all employees to be like loyal servants and make more contributions to me wholeheartedly. However, I am much smarter than them. Instead of ignoring the existence of employees, I will take them seriously. To be precise, I always put the employees who worked for me first in my mind.

From the bottom of my heart, I have no reason not to treat those employees who used their hands to accumulate my wealth well. I have no reason not to appreciate their efforts and sacrifices for me. Moreover, our world should have been filled full of warmth.

I love my employees. I never scold or insult them loudly, nor do I become domineering and indomitable in front of them like some rich folks do. What I provide my employees is warmth, equality, and tolerance. All these combined into one word is called respect. Respect for others is a need to satisfy our sense of morality, but I find that it is also an effective tool to motivate employees to work hard. The fact that every employee of Standard Oil does their best to work for the company makes me believe that: Give people the respect they deserve, and they can fully realize their potential.

The most basic aspect of human nature is the desire for generosity. I, myself, am thrifty and self-sufficient, but I never forget to help others generously. I remember that during the Great Depression, I borrowed several times to help those desperate friends, so that their factories and their families survived the crisis. And in my memory, I have never had a record of debt collection and forcing debts, because I know the value of tolerance.

As for the employees, I am equally generous and compassionate. Not only do I pay them higher salaries than any oil company, but I also allow them to enjoy the pension system that guarantees them a comfortable retirement. I also give them annual appointments with their bosses for Opportunities to raise their own salary. I do not deny the utilitarian effect of generosity, but I also know that my generosity will improve the living standards of employees, and this is precisely one of my duties. I hope that everyone who works for me will be rich because of me.

Employers are the guardians of employees, and my employees' problems are also my problems. I have the rights to choose. I can choose to ignore their needs or choose to meet their needs, but I like to choose the latter. I always try to understand what employees need, and then try to meet their needs. I keep asking them two questions: "What do you need?" and "How can I help?" I am always there to care for them. For me, one of the greatest joys of this position is that I can lend employees a hand.

Salaries and bonuses are quite attractive, but for some people, money does not trigger their motivation to serve, but paying attention can achieve this goal. In my opinion, everyone aspires to be considered valuable, valued, and respected by others. There is an invisible sign hanging on everyone's forehead, which says: Value me!

I cannot imagine the pain of being ignored at work or in the family. My goal is to make everyone feel good at work. Therefore, I am like a detective who wants to find clues to solve the case, constantly searching for the talents that each employee is proud of. When I understand the talents they think they are most worthy of, I will give them a heavier responsibility. An employer who is good at motivating employees to make the greatest contribution should never forget to mention that to letting employees see that following or being loyal to you is hopeful and promising, and giving attention and entrusting important tasks to them is also the key to motivate employees to work hard at work.

Being a kind, warm and considerate employer can make employees energetic and have high morales. But expressing gratitude to employees from time to time seems to be very useful. No employee will remember the bonus he received five years ago, but many people will always remember the kinds words of the employer and I will not hesitate to express my gratitude. Nothing has more influence than a timely and direct "thank you".

I like to leave a note paper on the desk of my subordinates with my words of thanks. The words of gratitude I wrote by hand for a minute or two may no longer be remembered. But my gratitude will have an inspiring impact. After so many years, they can still remember the warm encouragement left by their loving leader and regard it as a precious motto. This is a simple thank you statement and is also another proof of its great power.

I will definitely take my subordinates and their work or personal issues seriously. I understand that what everyone can contribute is limited, so when I try my best to solve problems for my subordinates, relatively, they can make more contributions.

John, now you are a leader. Your achievements come from your abilities and the abilities of your employees. I believe you should know how to do it.

Love,
Your Father

LETTER

36

Wealth is a form of responsibility

The greater the wealth, means the greater the responsibility.

Only fools are pretentious because they are rich.

Never let anyone with selfishness get a little benefit.

(With a good conscience our only sure reward, in hour of maximum danger, we do not shrink from this responsibility, we welcome it.)

November 20, 1907

Dear John:

I am very happy that a financial crisis that almost caused a national crisis has finally passed!

Now, I think our President, Theodore Roosevelt, can go to Louisiana to continue hunting with peace of mind, despite his surprising incompetence in this crisis. Of course, Mr. President did not do nothing. He supported Wall Street with "worries". God! Our taxpayer was so blind that he sent such a New Yorker into the White House.

Frankly speaking, the mention of Theodore Roosevelt's name and everything he did to Standard Oil makes me indignant. He is the narrowest and most vengeful villain I have ever seen. Yes, this villain succeeded. With the power in his hands, he became the winner of an unfair competition that was initiated by him. The federal court issued the huge fine that was unprecedented in American history and ordered its dissolution of our company. See what this despicable man has done to us!

However, I believe that his so-called punishment will not succeed after all, but he will feel greatly disappointed, because I believe that all our companies are not rubbish. We have an outstanding management team and sufficient funds. We can resist any risks and attacks; our wealth will come from their healthy bodies. Wait and see! There will be times when we secretly cheer.

However, we are indeed hurt and treated extremely unfairly. Theodore accused us of being a villain with huge wealth, and the judge insulted us as if we were notorious thieves, as if our wealth were conspired to plunder. Wrong! Those stupid guys do not know how big companies are built, and he does not want to know. Every cent of our money is permeated with our wisdom, and we have paid a load of sweat every step forward. The cornerstone of our business building is laid by our lives. But they do not want to listen, they want to be biased, only believing in their own inferior judgments, insulting our business ability, and even ignoring the fact that we use the cheapest and best quality kerosene to illuminate the United States.

I know that the long sword in Theodore's hand will definitely be swung until a big gain is achieved, because he rejected our proposal of reconciliation. But I am fearless, because I have a clear conscience, and the worst result is that he uses his power to break up our brilliant and happy family, but the happiness will not stop, and the glory will not fall. The future based on this reality will prove all this.

There is no doubt that we are undergoing an unprecedented persecution, from the Roosevelt administration. However, we cannot allow our emotions to interfere and use anger to suppress our conscience. When a crisis comes, we can never stand on the side-lines, it will make us feel ashamed and going against our conscience. We should come forward. Because we are citizens of the United States, we have a duty to save our country and our fellow citizens from disasters. As a rich man, I know that great wealth is also a great responsibility, and I shoulder the mission of benefitting mankind.

The financial crisis swept Wall Street. Depositors who were in panic lined up to withdraw their deposits from the bank. There was a run. When a crisis that would cause the US economy to enter the Great Depression again, I had a foreboding that the country had fallen into it. A Double crisis: the government lacks funds and the people lack confidence. At this moment, "Mr. Moneybag" must do something about this. I called Mr. Stone and asked the Associated Press to quote me and tell the American people: Our country never lacks credibility, and the scholars in the financial world pledge their credibility with their lives. If necessary, I would use half of the securities to help the country maintain its credibility. Please believe me, the financial earthquake will not happen.

Thank God, the crisis has passed, and Wall Street has come out of the predicament.

And for this moment, I did what I should do, as the Wall Street Journal commented, "Mr. Rockefeller helped Wall Street with his voice and huge sums of money." It is just that I will never let them know that in overcoming this panic, I was the one who took out the most money from my pocket, which makes me very proud.

Of course, Wall Street was able to successfully survive the credit crisis. Mr. Morgan can be described as outstanding. He is the outright commander of this war. He brought together a group of business celebrities to cope with the crisis and used his irreplaceable financial talents. The resolute personality saved Wall Street. So I said that the American people should thank him, the people on Wall Street should thank him, and Theodore Roosevelt should thank him even more, because Morgan did what Roosevelt should have done but failed to do because of his incompetence.

Nowadays, many people, and of course newspapers, praise the generous people, but to me it is worthless. The peace of conscience is the only reliable reward. The national crisis is the head, and we should do our part and have the courage to bear it. I think those people who sincerely extend a helping hand are just like me. We just want to shine our motherland with our own strength, faith, and loyalty.

But I am not without shameful records. Forty-six years ago, when so many young Americans obeyed the call of the motherland and went to the frontlines, loyally to fight for the liberation of slaves and the maintenance of the unity of the United States, as a young man, I had just opened the company and my family had to rely on it to live, thus, I did not participate in the war.

This may be a reassuring reason, but at that time the country needed me, and needed us to shed blood. This incident has always disturbed my conscience. It was not until the arrival of the economic crisis ten years ago that I had a chance at salvation. At that time, the federal government was unable to guarantee gold reserves, and Washington turned to Mr. Morgan for help, but Morgan was unable to do anything. It was, I, who put out a huge subsidy to the government to quell the financial panic. This makes me very happy, more than over how much money I make.

But I did not see myself as a saviour, let alone pretentious. Only fools are pretentious because of money. But because I am a citizen, that knows that I have huge wealth, and I also bear huge public responsibilities because of it. What is more noble than having huge wealth is to serve the motherland in accordance with the needs of the motherland.

John, we indeed have money, but at any time, we should not spend money arbitrarily. Our money is only used to create value for mankind, and we must not give any selfish people a little bit of benefit. Of course, we will never donate money to republicans to support their election campaigns anymore. Theodore Roosevelt has already hurt us.

Fame and virtue are the decoration of the soul. Without her, no matter how beautiful the body is, it should not be considered beautiful.

Love,
Your Father

LETTER
37

Enrich your mind

Even if you want to sell your soul, you have to sell it to yourself.

Let us learn to be smart and humble, humble and smart.

A great book is a great tree of wisdom, a great tree of mind.

(Let us then learn a wise humility, but at the same time a humble wisdom.)

August 1, 1914

Dear John:

Just like our physical appetite, we also have spiritual appetite. But many people often use the lack of time as an excuse to keep their hearts hungry, and only enrich them by accidents or by chance, but they never forget to satisfy their consumption below their necks.

Perhaps my view is a bit pessimistic. We are in an era where we continuously satisfy our needs below the neck but ignore the needs above the neck. In fact, you often hear people say: Missing a lunch is a big deal, but you never heard: When was the last time you satisfied your soul's hunger and thirst? Are we all spiritually rich? Obviously not.

In our world, people who are thirsty for spiritual energy can be seen everywhere. Those who live in depression, negativity, failure, and melancholy, they all desperately need spiritual nourishment and the call of inspiration, but almost all of them reject replenishing their hearts and instead let their hearts be dim.

It would be great if an empty mind could be like an empty belly, needing to be filled up to satisfy the owner. Unfortunately, there is no such thing, but to accept the punishment of spiritual emptiness.

The soul is the true home for each of us, and whether we are good or bad depends on her nurturing. Because everything that enters this true home has a function, it will be created to prepare for your future, or it will be destroyed, reducing your possible future life achievements. For example, positivity.

Every top-notch person who reaches the peak or is almost reaching the peak is positive. They are positive because they regularly enrich their hearts with good, clean, powerful, and positive spiritual thoughts. Just as food is the nutrition of the body, they do not forget their daily spiritual food. They know that if they can fill the upper part of the neck, they will never worry about filling the lower part of the neck, or even worry about the financial problems of old age.

One must find one's own home, so as not to wander or become a beggar. First of all, even if you want to sell your soul, you have to sell it to yourself. We have to accept ourselves. We must be clear that man was created with God's own mind and our status is second only to angels. God will not set any apparent restrictions on age, education, gender, fatness, skin color, height, or any other superficial limits. God also has no time to create useless people, let alone ignore everyone. Second, we must have a positive attitude.

Two years ago, when Mr. Carl Jung and I met unexpectedly, the psychologist told me a story: a man was trapped by a flood, and he had to climb to the roof to take refuge. Someone among the neighbours floated over and said, "John, the water is really terrible this time, isn't it?"

John replied, "No, it's not that bad."

The neighbour was a little surprised, so he retorted, "How can you say that? Your chicken coop has been washed away."

John said, "Yes, I know, but I started raising ducks six months ago, and now they are all swimming nearby. Everything is fine."

"But, John, this time the water ruined your crops," the neighbour insisted.

John replied: "No. The crops I planted were damaged due to lack of water. Just last week, someone told me that my land needs more water, so it's solved now."

The pessimistic neighbour once again said to the smiling John: "But look, John, the water is still rising. It's about to rise to the level of your window."

The optimistic John smiled happily and said: "I hope so, these windows are really dirty and need to be cleaned."

This sounds like a joke. But obviously this is a realm—deciding to adopt a positive attitude to deal with this complex, ups and downs of this world. Once this state is reached, even in negative situations, we can make the mind automatically respond positively. In order to achieve this state, we can only enrich and cleanse our hearts.

Everyone can change or be changed. Mr. Jung said that as long as a person changes his vocabulary, he can build his income, his enjoyment, and improve his life, and even change his life. For example, the word "hate" should be removed from your vocabulary. Do not think about it but replace it with the word "love" for writing, feeling and dreaming. Obviously, the words to be removed and replaced are almost endless, but the mind will become purer and more positive from the removal.

Our minds act on the things that supply her. I believe that what I put in my heart is very important to my future. So, the question is obviously: how do we feed our souls – when do we find spiritual food.

Have you ever heard that the lumberjack's output will decline, just because he did not spare time to sharpen him and his axe? We spend money, and a lot of time, to modify the appearance of the mind, shave, and trim our hair. Can we spend the same time and money to make up the inner part of the mind? Of course, there is, and it can be done.

In fact, spiritual food is available everywhere, such as books. There are no books written through great spiritual impacts that are not food that washes and enriches our hearts. They have already pointed out the direction for future generations once and for all, and we can choose whatever we want. A great book is a great tree of wisdom, a great tree of mind, in which we will be reshaped. Let us learn to be smart and humble, humble and smart.

Of course, we should not read books written for businessman by businessmen. Their books are like a plague, spreading shameless evil thoughts, corrupt news, and arrogant stupidity. Their books are only worthy of those shallow and vulgar people. What we need is a book that can bring us the confidence and strength to act, can push our life to a new height, and guide us to do good. For example, "Pushing to the Front" by Orison Swett Marden.

It is great work that stirs our souls and stimulates our passion for life. I believe that the American people will benefit from its appearance, and therefore use their own power in the most positive ways to reach the dream of life. I even believe that whoever misses the opportunity to read it is likely to miss the great life. I hope my children and grandchildren can read this book. It can open the door to happiness for all people.

The driving force that led people to climb to the peak is a driving force that is maintained and emphasized regularly and is growing stronger. Those who have a successful life can undoubtedly realize that there is a lot of space in the peak, but there is not enough space for people to sit and stay. They understand that the mind, like the body, must be given regular nutrition. Physical, mental, and spiritual nutrition must be taken care of separately.

John, no one can block our way home unless we do not want to come back. Let the light of the soul shine on our way forward.

Love,
Your Father

LETTER

38

(Part 1)
Anyone can be a great man
We must be the salt of the world.

People are nothing great, but there is nothing greater than people.

(Men are great only on their intrinsic value, and not on the position they may incidentally happen to occupy.)

June 8, 1906

Dear John:

There is a holy saying in the Gospel of Matthew: "You are the salt of the world."

This metaphor is ordinary and thought-provoking. Salt has a taste, but also cleans and preserves food. Christ wanted to teach his disciples what mission they should shoulder and what influence they should exert. They came to the world to purify and beautify the world they are in. They want to protect the world from corruption and give the world fresher and a healthier life.

The primary responsibility of salt is to have a salty taste. The salty taste of salt symbolizes a noble, powerful, and truly religious life. So, what should we use our wealth, principles, and beliefs for? Undoubtedly, we must be the salt of the world, actively serve the society, and benefit the world. This is each of us and the last social responsibility.

Our responsibility now is to dedicate ourselves completely to the world and people around us, and to concentrate on our art of giving. I do not think there is anything greater than this.

Speaking of greatness, I remembered a great speech, which is rare in my life. It tells me that people are nothing great, but there is nothing greater than people. It depends on what you have done for your compatriots and your country.

Now, I will transcribe this great speech to you, and hope it will be of great benefit to you.

Love,
Your Father

LETTER

38

(Part 2)
The Speech

Ladies and gentlemen:

I am honoured to have met some important people here today. Although you will say that there are no big people in this city, big people are all born in London, San Francisco, Rome or other big cities, and not from the local area, they all come from outside this town. If so, you are very wrong. The fact is that there are as many big people here as with other cities. There are many big names in the audience, including men and women.

Now, allow me to boldly say that the biggest mistake we often make when judging whether a person is a big person is that we always think that big people have spacious offices. However, I want to tell you that this world does not know what kind of person the greatest person in the world is.

So, who is the greatest man in the world? Young people may be anxious to ask such questions. Let me tell you that a greatest man is not necessarily someone who has an office in a high-rise building. The reason why a person is known for being the greatest man, lies in his value and has nothing to do with the position he has obtained. Who can say that a king who lives on food is greater than a farmer who works hard? However, please do not blame young people who hold a certain public office and think they may become big shots.

Now, I would like to ask everyone here, who of you plans to be a great person?

That guy in a western cowboy hat, you said you will become a big man in this city someday, really?

When are you going to realize this wish?

You said that when another war broke out, you would charge into battle in the rain of bullets and pull down the enemy's flag from the flagpole. You would wear a medal on your chest, return to the country triumphantly, and serve as a public office awarded to you by the government. Become a big shot!

No, it will not! Young man, you are not really great in doing this, but we should not blame your ideas. You were taught this way when you were in school. Those who hold official positions have participated in the war bravely.

I remember that when the Spanish War in the United States just ended, there was a peace parade in our city. People told me that when the parade team walked on Blow Street, a carriage stopped at the gate of my house. Sitting in the carriage was Mr. Hobson. Everyone threw their hats into the sky, waved their handkerchiefs, and shouted: "Long live Hopson!" If I were there, I would shout like that, because he deserves this great honour.

But, suppose I go to the university forum tomorrow and ask everyone: "Boys, who sank the USS Merrimac?" If they answer: "It's Hobson." Then their answer is a seven-eighth lie, because there were a total of eight people who sank the USS Merrimac, and the other seven people had been exposed to Spanish artillery fire because of their positions. As the commander, Mr. Hopson was probably out of the artillery fire.

My friends, the audience here tonight are all intellects, but I dare say that none of you can tell who the seven people are fighting with Mr. Hopson.

Why do we use this method to teach history? We must teach the students that no matter how low a person's position is, as long as he performs his duties, the American people should give him as much honour as a king.

Most people teach their children in this way. Her young son asked, "Mom, what is that tall building?"

"That is the tomb of General Grant."

"Who is General Grant?"

"He is the one who put down the rebellion."

How can history be taught like this? Think about it, everyone, if we only have one General Grant, will the war be won? Oh, no. So why build a grave on the Hudson River? That is not because General Grant himself was a great man. The tomb was built there because he was a representative figure, representing two hundred thousand heroic soldiers who lost their lives to the country, and many of them were as great as General Grant. This is the real reason that beautiful tomb stands on the banks of the Hudson River.

I remember one thing that can be used to illustrate this situation, and this is the only example I can think of tonight. I am ashamed of this incident and cannot forget it. I close my eyes now and go back to 1863. I can see my home in the Berkshire Hills, the bull market is full of people, and the local church and city hall are also full.

I heard the band playing, saw the national flag flying, and the handkerchief waving in the wind. I still have fresh memories of that day. The crowd is here to welcome a company of soldiers, and that company is also coming in line. After serving one period of military service in the Civil War, they have to extend another period. They are now being welcomed by their hometown elders. I was just a young guy, but I was the company commander. On that day, I was triumphant, like a fully inflated balloon—just a thin needle could pierce me. I am at the forefront of the team; I am prouder than anyone in the world.

We lined up into the city hall. They arranged for my soldiers to sit in the middle of the hall, and I sat in the front row. Then the town officials lined up out of the crowd. They walked to the stage and sat in a semicircle. Next, the mayor could not sit in the centre of the semi-circular seat. He is an old man with grey hair and has never held a public office before. He believes that since he holds a public office, he is a great man. When he stood up, he first adjusted his heavy glasses, and then looked around the people under the stage with an extremely majestic posture. Suddenly, his eyes fell on me, and then the kind old man walked to me and invited me to sit down with the officials in the town.

Invited me to the stage! Before I joined the army, no city official noticed me. I sat in front of the stage and let my sabre hang on the floor. I put my arms around my chest, waiting to be welcomed, and feel like Napoleon V! Pride always comes before destruction and failure.

At this time, the mayor delivered a speech on behalf of the people, welcoming our group of soldiers who had returned triumphantly. He took out the speech from his pocket, carefully spread it out on the lecture table, and adjusted his glasses. He took a few steps from behind the pulpit, and then moved forward. He must have studied the speech manuscript very carefully, because he adopted the posture of a speaker, placing the weight of his body on his left foot, moving his right foot slightly forward, retracting his shoulders, and then opening his mouth with his hand at an angle of forty-five degrees.

"Dear citizens," he said, "We are very happy to welcome these brave fighters... who are not afraid of bleeding... the soldiers have returned to their hometowns. We are especially happy to see those who are with us today. There is a young hero (referring to me)... This young hero, in our imagination, we have seen him lead troops in desperate fights against the enemy. We saw his shiny sabre... shining brightly in the sun, and he shouted at his troops, "Charge!""

God! This kind old man knew nothing about war. If he knew a little more about war, he would know the fact that it is a grave mistake for an infantry officer to run ahead of his subordinates at a dangerous moment. I even held the command knife that was gleaming in the sun and shouted to my subordinates: Charge! I have never done this before.

Think about it, will I run to the front and be attacked by the enemy in front and leave the troops behind? The officer should not go there. In actual combat, the officer's position is behind the soldier. Because I was a staff officer, when the rebels rushed out of the woods and attacked us from all directions, I always rode a horse and shouted to our army all the way: "The officers, retreat! The officers, retreat!" Then, every officer will retreat to the back of the combat zone, and the higher the rank, the further away. This is not because he lacks courage, but because the rules of battle are like this. If the general ran to the front and was killed, the battle would definitely be lost, because the entire battle plan is in his mind and he must be in absolute safety.

I was even holding "that sabre gleaming in the sun". What?! Among the soldiers sitting in the city hall that day, there were people who had used their lives to protect me, a half-sized officer, and someone that carried me across the deep river. Some people were not there because they died for the country. The speaker also mentioned them, but they were not noticed. Yes, those who really died for the country were not noticed, but this little boy of me, was said to be the hero of the time.

Why am I treated as a hero? It is simple, because the speaker fell into the same stupid trap. This little boy is an officer, the others are just soldiers. I learned a lesson that I will never forget. A person is great not because he has a certain official title. The reason why he is great is that he used a few tools to create a greater cause and accomplish his life goal as an unknown civilian. This is the real greatness.

As long as an individual can provide the public with spacious streets, comfortable houses, elegant schools, solemn churches, sincere admonitions, and genuine happiness, as long as he can get the gratitude of local residents, no matter where he goes, he is great. But if he is not thanked by the local residents, no matter where he goes to the earth, he will not be a great person.

I hope everyone here knows that we should live in meaningful actions, not years; we live in feelings, not the numbers on the phone buttons; we live in thoughts, not air; The time should be calculated based on the beating of the heart under the correct goal.

If you forget what I said tonight, please do not forget the following statement: The person who thinks the most, feels the noblest, acts the most righteous, and lives the most fulfilling life.